EYES UP

ALEXANDRA V. HOOVER

EYES UP

How to Trust God's Heart by Tracing His Hand

FOREWORD BY DR. DERWIN L. GRAY

B&H
PUBLISHING
NASHVILLE, TENNESSEE

978-1-0877-4712-5

Published by B&H Publishing Group
Nashville, Tennessee

Dewey Decimal Classification: 248.84
Subject Heading: GRACE (THEOLOGY) / CHRISTIAN LIFE /
SELF-REALIZATION

To my children, Leilla, Kingston, and Sophia.
My whole heart.
I wrote this book in the margins of our lives. As I
loved and cared for you. As our family found our
footing in the midst of a pandemic and challenges.
You have always helped me remember what love is.
You are my greatest Ebenezers.
I pray you taste the goodness of God through these
words, that they might one day be an Ebenezer to
you. When you lose sight of God's hand or heart,
remember them.
Keep your *eyes up*.

Acknowledgments

Mario, thank you for fighting for me when I couldn't fight for myself.

To the friends who carried me through, thank you.

To Pastor Derwin and Vicki, and the rest of the Transformation Church family, thank you.

To Ashley and to Meredith, thank you.

To Ms. Carpenter, Ms. Jarussi, Pastor Jeffries, and Angela Magee, thank you.

To my mom, thank you for love, for strength, for hope.

To the Father, the Son, and the Holy Spirit—this is Yours, thank you.

May these words be an Ebenezer to the goodness of God for us all.

Contents

Foreword

Thirty thousand dollars for rocks! You've got to be kidding me. Thirty grand for a gravel parking lot." Those were my words to the pavement company we brought out to give us a quote for the future parking lot of our fledging church plant.

My wife Vicki and I did not grow up in church. We came to faith in our mid-twenties, so we found it odd that the nightclubs we used to party in looked more like the multiethnic scene from the book of Revelation than Jesus's church on Earth.

> And they sang a new song:
> You are worthy to take the scroll
> and to open its seals,
> because you were slaughtered,
> and you purchased people
> for God by your blood
> from every tribe and language
> and people and nation.
> You made them a kingdom
> and priests to our God,
> and they will reign on the earth.
> (Rev. 5:9–10)

In response to God's call, we set out to plant Transformation Church, a multiethnic, multigenerational, mission-shaped community that loves God completely, ourselves correctly, and our neighbors compassionately. As we were attempting to plant Transformation Church, discouragement and doubt surrounded us. Other pastors told me that a multiethnic church would never work, especially in South Carolina, and there is a reason Sunday morning is the most segregated time in America. Not only did we have this discouragement, but being told that a parking lot full of rocks would cost $30,000, we were just about done.

During this tumultuous time, my wife had a dream. In the dream, the owner of the pavement company said to my wife, "Are you and Derwin still trying to start that new church?" She said, "Yes, but we are running into some financial difficulty." Then he said, "Well, if you are still planning to start the church, my wife and I prayed, and God told us to donate the parking lot for free." Then she woke up.

A few weeks passed and I was coaching my son's flag football team. After the game, the owner of the pavement company, whose son was on the team, asked Vicki, "Are you and Derwin still trying to start that new church?" She said, "Yes, but we are running into some financial difficulty." Then he said, "Well, if you are still planning to start the church, my wife and I prayed, and God told us to donate the parking lot for free." We both just wept. And wept. And wept.

Over the last twelve years, Jesus has empowered the people of Transformation Church to do some epic things. More than 7,000 people have come to faith through the ministry; one Christmas we paid off $4,000,000 of medical debt for people in the state of South Carolina. God has been spectacular among us.

Times have been tough. Gut-wrenching disappointments. Global pandemics. Divisive times. In moments like these, when times get tough, doubt creeps in, and discouragement surrounds me, I open a drawer in my office and I grab a stone. The stone I grab is one of the original stones that was in our old gravel parking lot when we first started Transformation Church. That stone reminds me of God's *presence, power, provision,* and *providence.* That stone is my "Ebenezer," which means "stone of help" or "stone of a warrior" (1 Sam. 7:12).

The book you are about to read was written by Alexandria Hoover. Alex is a living stone, a precious jewel in King Jesus's crown of mercy. The Spirit of God brought Alex, her husband, and two young children to Transformation Church when she was only twenty-five years old. Immediately, her love for Jesus, her family, Jesus's church, and discipleship was clear. She quickly joined our staff.

When I think of Alex, the words that come to mind are disciple of Jesus, wife, mother, daughter, survivor, warrior, and ministry leader. As her pastor, I could not be prouder of her. She has listened and learned well. She has lived well. As the pages of her book unfold, her life will unfold before you; and more than that, so will plenty of wisdom from Scripture. As you walk beside her in this book, learning how to chart your own Ebenezer journey with God, you will see that Jesus our Cornerstone is *present,* unleashing His *power,* His *provision,* and creating trust with His *providence.* Her writing is transparent, vulnerable, raw, and thoroughly biblical. You will learn about each stone God has built in your story—even when you didn't have eyes to see them before—and how each of these stones are essential if you want to live a life of abundance.

This book itself will be an Ebenezer stone in your life.

Eyes up, friend. There is so much of Jesus to see and experience.

Dr. Derwin L. Gray

Cofounder and lead elder-pastor of Transformation Church and author of *God Do You Hear Me?*, *The Good Life*, and *How to Heal the Racial Divide: What the Bible Says, and the First Christians Knew, about Racial Reconciliation*

@DerwinLGray

Introduction

My family and I live in North Carolina, and there's this beautiful greenway not too far from Charlotte that we love. We've seen it change over the years, growing into a soft place to land for those looking for rest and reprieve. It has the most whimsical creek and wooden-rope bridge that, when we stride across it, makes us all feel like we are characters in the cast of Disney's *Peter Pan*. No matter what time of year it is, when we are looking for rest, you can probably find us in that place.

And this time was no different. We were enduring the first year of the pandemic that changed everyone's life, and to find a sense of comfort, we took to the outside world.

Water, wildlife, blue skies—they have a way of grounding me and helping me remember that although I may feel out of control, and am, God is not. They point me to the uncreated Creator, who hung the stars and called them each by name. The One that took the time to care for you and me. And that always feels like good news, no matter what kind of year or day I'm having.

On this day, though, we decided to go down a trail we'd never been on before. The greenway wasn't too intimidating, so I thought, *Why not take a different path, and see where it leads us?* Call me an amateur, or naïve, but I thought the trail signs would be enough.

They weren't. You know why? Because I'd been looking at the wrong signposts. My gaze had landed in the wrong place, which gave me no perspective on where I actually was, and eventually led me the wrong direction. In the end, I had to cast my eyes to the right signposts to gain a sense of perspective, and when I did, I could finally make out the direction where we were supposed to be going.

The whole time I felt sort of like Bilbo Baggins, that hobbit invented by J. R. R. Tolkien, when he and his mates wandered into a dark, cursed forest. Do you remember how the story goes in *The Hobbit*? Gandalf, a good wizard, is sure that Bilbo is the man for the job, and directs Bilbo and his hobbit friends to go on a noble mission to reclaim their kingdom. That's all well and good until they stumble into a deep, dark wood that is designed to intentionally confuse them. (Oh, and by the way, it's full of giant spiders. NO THANK YOU.)

The longer the hobbits wander inside of the cursed forest, the more they can't distinguish up from down, down from up, right from left, or left from right. They cannot remember the correct path. They even turn on each other in their delusional state.

Have you ever been there? Lost, scared, disoriented, paranoid, irritable? Those hobbits understand. If you remember how the scene goes down, they look for clues of hope all around them. Heads turning right and left, they look for a way out. Eyes casted down at the soil and the roots they stumble over, they get lost in their own thoughts. *Surely this is the right path. Or is it that one? Wait, we've been here before. Or have we not? These surroundings are terrible. How did I even end up in this place? Why did I even sign up for this mission? Why did I trust Gandalf? Why are any of us even here? None of this makes any sense. None of these people I'm on the mission with understand me—I don't even understand me right now! Is there even a way out of this? I should have never even come on this journey to begin with. I should just turn back.*

After enough time in the dark woods, with scary circumstances at every turn, Bilbo and his friends can barely see any more and *they almost give up.*

Why?

Because looking *around* in a cursed environment is only going to make you go in circles, eyes darting around to this circumstance and the next. Unable to escape. Unable to press forward. Unable to find the right way. Unable to believe.

But eventually, everything changes when Bilbo's eyes wander somewhere.

Up.

So simple and profound. Bilbo stops looking *around* for evidence of hope and just . . . looks up. What does he see? A tree. One that gives him a way out of the endless circles, doubting, darkness, and disorientation.

And so he climbs up, and up, and up, and eventually he reaches the top of the tree and emerges from the darkness, into the light above the forest, staring at a clear sky and the tops of a million other trees.

From this new vantage point, he can finally see clearly. He can see obvious evidence of where they've been—of the progress they've made, even when it felt like they hadn't been making any progress—and he can even see where they are going.

Lost before, now Bilbo is grounded and oriented toward the right direction. In a moment his back was against the wall and he felt lost, he now has renewed faith in the direction of Gandalf, in the people he was with, and in the mission he was called to.

All this fresh faith, simply because he lifted his eyes up.

There's this famous pastor from the nineteenth century, Charles Spurgeon, who was quite the wordsmith. In 1867, he apparently said something to this effect in a sermon:

"God is too good to be unkind and He is too wise to be mistaken. And when we cannot trace His hand, we must trust His heart." (Truth be told, if we track backward all the way to his original words, they were spoken just a little bit differently than this famous quote he is given credit for, but the heart of what he's saying is pretty close to this!)[1]

Hear me say this: I'm with Spurgeon on what he said. There will be times we can't trace God's hand, and when we can't, yes, *we must trust His heart.*

But there are also plenty of times we can trace God's hand. And you know what? The Bible gives us a way to do that. When we're lost in a cursed, broken world, turning our head left and right, going around in circles, disoriented by our circumstances and doubts—wondering if God has ever really shown up for us, wondering if His direction in our life was real to begin with, wondering if His people or His mission is really worth it, wondering if His goodness or His heart is even something that should be trusted at all—the Bible gives us a direction to look that has the power to change our entire perspective. The Bible gives us something to climb up on, and *remember* just how far we've come, and where we're going. The Bible gives us a way to see clearly how God has, *actually and really and for sure,* shown up for us till now—which gives us fresh trust that He'll do it again. And when we take the Bible up on this offer, we emerge on the other side with renewed faith in the direction of God over our lives, in the people we are on the journey with, and in the mission we've been called to.

The direction Bilbo looked is the same direction we must look: up. But what we'll cast our eyes upon isn't a tree—it's a stone. Something the Bible calls an *Ebenezer stone.* And friend, you have no idea how many Ebenezer stones are in your journey. But let me tell you: *they are there.*

The purpose of an Ebenezer stone? To trace the places God showed up. To prove to you that God isn't just good, He is good *to you.* To give you obvious evidence that God *has* met you, even when it seemed at some point before now that He hadn't. To pull you out of the fog that immediately surrounds you and lift you upward.

Wild as it sounds, the reverse of what Spurgeon says is also true. As it turns out, one of the ways to trust God's heart—and trust that He'll show up in our life, whether that life is straight-up crazy right now or just crazy-normal—is to trace how His hand has moved before.

Problem is, we can't see how has His hand has moved when we're stuck in the shadows or fumbling our way through a fallen, cursed world that often confuses us. We can't stay fixated on our immediate circumstances. We have to be willing to look up—to *go* up.

Are you willing?

I hope with all my heart that your answer is yes. Because friend, if you are willing to look up at the stones God has built in your life (more on what that means in the coming pages), I can promise you this: you'll come out on the other side of this book with a clear lay of your life's landscape, and you'll be able to trace *exactly* where God has moved in your life, and the mission He's taking you on in your future. You'll be convinced that God is good, and *he's good to you.*

All because you were simply willing to cast your eyes up. All because you dared to trace His hand in your life—even in the places you thought He wasn't there and He didn't care.

So I'll ask you again: are you willing? Do you dare?

If the answer is yes, then buckle up, friend, because it's time to climb. Oh, and prepare to make a lot of stops, because there are a lot of stones God that has built in your journey with Him. And I don't want you to miss a single one of them.

Don't you look down. Don't you cast your gaze on the soil and the roots that trip you up. Don't you get lost in the fog of your circumstances. *Eyes up.*

Amen?

1 | The Starting Stone
Where Were You, God?

When I was a little girl, I would write small notes on ripped-up college-ruled paper. The kind that had the faded blue lines when it would sit under the sun far too long. A brown-haired, brown-eyed little girl of the 90s, I was probably around six when I began writing them. My mom had cut my hair to some sort of a long bob that I absolutely hated, and given that I was a poster child for the 90s, I'm pretty sure I was wearing some sort of oversized sweater.

I wasn't a writer yet. I was a thinker, a dreamer, a little girl with a deep soul who carried both strong love and profound pain. I had words stirring up in me, and the only way to process my life was through them. I'd rip up the notebook paper into palm-sized notes. The jagged edges of the paper told a story of themselves, too. I needed the notes to be a specific size—big enough to carry my hard days and dreams, small enough to keep tucked away in my corduroy pants.

I wrote in the margins of my life.

For starters, I'd always write in my unique Ikea bunk bed, after school, hiding from the fuss of life. This was my favorite spot. I was in my private world up in that wooden haven. Unbothered by the circumstances of life, dreaming of what could be, wondering when the dreams would come. I'd been begging for the wooden bunk bed with the light oak finish for a long time, every time we visited Ikea. Something about it was magical. Did it remind me of the "could be" dreams? I had been eyeing the loft bunk bed with the desk underneath for as long as I could remember. Somehow my mom was able to gather enough money to bring it home.

There were other writing spaces of choice. Like the back seat of my mother's car during our extended bumper-to-bumper traffic-jam waits. Or at the table while dinner was cooking, the smell of Venezuelan spices filling the air. Or the hallways of my mother's second job, as I hid from the coworkers who lacked compassion for a single mother and the life we were thrown into.

There had always been something healing and unique when it came to carving out precious time for my words. I'd run to my room, plop down on my oversized beanbag, and unpack the burdens of the day—secrets, hopes, and dreams.

I suppose I was allowing space for my heart to breathe. Somehow life had invited me into this space of words, breaking, and healing. As I wrote, most of the days, hope and wonder carried me through. I felt at home, at peace. Even in the hard moments of life, writing invited me into the nuance of the human heart. I could feel the weight my mother was under. The tension was so thick that it took the breath from my lungs, leaving me exasperated, gasping for oxygen.

I would try to breathe through it. But it wasn't enough. I needed some other outlet, so I would go to my room and climb that beautiful oak bed, rip up a page, and start unleashing days' worth of feelings. I loved giving my heart space to breathe out doubt and breathe in hope (something I'd come to enjoy later in life in much fuller ways).

Often the thoughts would come so fast that my writing would end up being passion-filled scribbles that only I could understand. They were thoughts I kept mostly to myself, full of questions, anguish, despair, and rejection. After all, I was a little girl who was consistently told she was too much, whose words were not welcomed, whose Venezuelan accent was used as a weapon against her brown skin and brown hair. Defeat and confusion became a common theme in her little notes, but somehow, hope lived there too, though I couldn't tell you why.

The thought of a better day consumed me. I would write down even the smallest joys. I had somehow, even at such a tender age, learned to see the beauty in the broken things, the signposts of new seasons, the peace found in car rides with my mom with the windows rolled down. I'd think to myself, *We're going to be okay. We've been here before but have pressed on. We will be okay.* Those notes—held in a little wooden box in the first drawer of my dresser and also holding my heart together—I now know they were more like prayers.

Words have always followed me. Even though they've often been clumsy, they're always the best gift, helping me name my seasons, aches, and life. They have helped me trace life and take account of it. They were whispers to the Father before I even knew that He was listening. They carried me into hope and joy. They stored the places where I saw victory and defeat. They served as a holding place and a carrier for my thoughts and feelings. They carried me from season to season, helping me remember that not all was always hard. They also held a special place of connection with my mom. I'd often write her letters, little notes in dark and difficult seasons: notes of apology, notes of encouragement, hopeful words, and even my grievances. Sometimes I'd even write to myself, or to God.

Dear Mom, I'm sorry that I had an attitude today. I know things are hard right now. I love you. You are a great mom. Love, Alexandra

Why does it have to be this way?

God, my grandmother tells me that You are real, but I don't see You. Are You real? If You are, can You please help us?

As I look back on my faith journey, I now see those notes for what they were: they were my starting stones, as I like to say. You've got some sort of starting stone in your journey too, you know, although yours may not look like note-prayers.

But I've gotten ahead of myself.

Let's start with what I mean by stones.

The God Who Remembers

The book of 1 Samuel in the Bible holds a story that has always grabbed my attention. It takes place during a transition period—between the time the people of God were led by judges and the time they were led by kings. They didn't know they'd need a prophet to help guide this transition, but God knew.

But the book doesn't start with the prophet God provides for them. Instead, the book starts by introducing us to one of my favorite Bible friends, Hannah. She's a praying woman. A woman who dedicated her life to God. She followed Him, sought Him, and loved Him. From what we read about her, she lived a life of gratitude. She was known for her commitment and conviction even while her prayers seemed to remain unanswered. She also lived a life of affliction and pain, showing us all what it looks like to hold space for the tension of both grief and wild hope. Isn't that something? That hope in God can coexist with the pain brought on by our circumstances? Even in her fallenness, Hannah felt both and carried both. But ultimately she let one lead her.

Hannah was one of Elkahan's wives. *Did you say one of multiple wives, Alex?* I know. Stay with me. We're talking about a certain time period and cultural context in the Old Testament, thousands of years ago, when it was common for men to have more than one wife. We could camp out there for a while and explore some things, but for the sake of time, let's hear how Hannah's story plays out.

Peninnah, Elkahan's other wife, had children. Our friend Hannah had been unable to conceive for years. The pain that followed her was often unbearable, so much so that the priest Eli assumed she was drunk from the utter brokenness and weeping and wailing that she brought to the Lord at the temple (1 Sam. 1:10, 12–14).

In a culture that prized having kids as the primary badge of honor for women, Hannah was shamed for not being able to bear children; she was looked down on and, most likely, even talked about as gossip spread through town about her condition. Scripture says her "rival," the other wife, even taunted her, making fun of her inability to bring little ones into the world (1 Sam. 1:5–7). Can you hear the whispers around town? *Still no kids? Goodness, God must be cursing her. I wonder what she did to make Him mad. I wonder what's wrong with her.*

As I think about her story, I can relate. Hannah was faithful yet overlooked. She showed up and gave all that she had, yet life handed her a different set of cards. She was committed and wanted nothing more than to give God the glory. Yet there she was—childless, alone, and accused.

When we feel like God overlooks us, it leaves us wondering if His kindness was ever ours to have. "This isn't fair. Does He choose favorites? Am I doing this wrong, the faith? Maybe I'm just not believing enough."

Scripture tells us that Hannah was weeping, heartbroken over the circumstance she found herself in (1 Sam. 1:7, 10). I have uttered prayers like that before. Prayers that only the Father can understand. Prayers so deep and personal that they were more like groans than actual words. Groans that communicate the ache and depth of my petitions, my agony. Words that can only be unpacked and unraveled by Him. I want to go back and tell Hannah that I understand her. That I, too, have felt forgotten and overlooked. Why on earth does it seem that the goodness of God picks favorites? Why does Peninnah draw an Ace every time while we Hannahs of the world always get dealt a bad hand?

In the eyes of her culture and even her priest, Hannah was a lost cause, a forgotten face in a sea of other women whose lives were full of blessing. She was invisible to everyone around her. *Everyone except God.* Scripture tells us that God remembered her (1 Sam. 1:19). He'd heard her. He'd seen her.

I'd be silly not to stop there and let that settle into our souls. I remember the first time I read the story, those words struck a heartstring, a chord. For some reason, the fact that God had met Hannah in such a personal way absolutely overwhelmed me. "The Lord remembered her."

Gosh, I thought. *I want to be remembered. I want to remember hope and joy. I want to know this hope and joy that meet us when we're remembered by someone, by God.*

Do I get to be remembered?

God, why don't I feel remembered?

Why do I feel the complete opposite?

Why do I feel like You've forgotten me?

And then I retraced Hannah's steps. What did she do when she felt forgotten?

> Deeply hurt, Hannah prayed to the LORD and wept with many tears. Making a vow, she pleaded, "LORD of Armies, if you will take notice of your servant's affliction, remember and not forget me, and give your servant a son, I will give him to the LORD all the days of his life, and his hair will never be cut."
> (1 Sam. 1:10–11)

I felt Hannah's ache right along with her. But you know what? I felt her hope, too, in the undercurrent of her prayer.

Her faith became mine. She let me borrow some of it. She helped me go to God in my pain. She helped me show up to His presence with all my agony and reach out for His fatherly compassion. God helps us along that way, doesn't He? In stories like Hannah's, He helps us see those around us press on, and it gives us the hope to keep going.

We are not forgotten. You are not forgotten. God's kindness and faithfulness make a way for us to experience life and love. We don't serve a forgetful God but a faithful God. One who sees and hears and remembers us. What may look like His inactivity will almost always be our inability to see His activity—to see His grace, His heart, His hand at work. This is why our gaze matters so much. What we set our eyes on becomes our source of hope and direction. Hannah knew where to look, not to the naysayers or the crumbling circumstances but at Him.

What did a lifted gaze look like for her? It looked like her resolve to keep going back to the temple even when God's activity and ability to move seemed absent. *She remembered who God was over what her circumstances told her.* This temple was a visible reminder that God was with her. Day after day, she kept her eyes fixed on it; she kept going back in remembrance of the goodness of God. She kept showing up, knowing that *God was in that room somehow,* and that somehow, someway, *He'd meet her here and help her.* People don't pray to the point that Hannah did unless they believe that. And this hope carried her to the next day.

See, Hannah let God's character carve the guardrails of her faith. He was good, and He was good to her—in the midst of the pain and even when it didn't feel like He was. Hannah's hope in God's heart carried her when she couldn't see God's hand. It was His heart that she had resolved herself in, not her circumstances.

That right there is its own miracle.

But then something beautiful happens: Hannah gives birth to a son named Samuel and immediately dedicates Him to the Lord—meaning, she gives Samuel to the current priest (Eli) so that he would join the priesthood (1 Sam. 1: 20–28). And what's the priesthood, you ask? A people set apart from the rest of the Israelites to mediate between them and God. The son that Hannah so desperately prayed for was to be a conduit of hope and deliverance for so many of the Israelites. Her pain had produced deep perseverance for us all to glean from and a purpose for all to prosper from—for our good and His glory. As the temple reminded her of God's kindness and help, now here is a son, another reminder. A living reminder. God is here, and He is good. For Hannah, God answered her prayer and gave her a son, Samuel. For us, our greatest gift and reminder that the Lord is for us and with us is a son, too—the Son of God. Jesus. We were in agony, in darkness, in accusation, in shame, just like Hannah. And just like Hannah, God remembered us in that place, and sent down a Son who could change things.

The Ebenezer Stone: A Way to Remember God

Fast-forward a lot of years, and we find Samuel has grown up. And, lo and behold, we find that he wasn't just an answer to Hannah's prayer; he was also an answer to Israel's need for a trustworthy prophet and judge who could transition them into the time period of the kings, where he would one day appoint two of Israel's first kings. When we find him in 1 Samuel 7, a few things have happened:

1. God has officially called him and made him a prophet. *Yay. Good.*
2. The ark of the covenant (the tangible sign of God's power and presence) has been captured by the Philistines, enemies of God's people, and then returned back to Jerusalem. *Oh no. But yay that it's back!*
3. The people have been living in idolatry, following after many other gods, but finally long for the Lord again. *Uh-oh. Worshipping other gods? Not good.*
4. The Philistines may have given the ark back, but they aren't gone. *Do I hear foreboding music in the background? Yes, yes I do.*

That's right. In 1 Samuel 7, the Philistines are back, ready to fight God's people, and they are a formidable enemy. So Samuel tells them this: "If you are returning to the LORD with all your heart, get rid of the foreign gods and the Ashtoreths that are among you, set your hearts on the LORD, and worship only him. Then he will rescue you from the Philistines" (1 Sam. 7:3).

And you know what? They do. The nation repents of their sin, destroys their idols, and begins to seek the Lord (1 Sam. 7:2–4). They stop looking up to their idols, and they finally look up to God. Samuel gathers the people at Mizpah to confess their sin and offer a sacrifice on their behalf (vv. 5–9).

Here's the crazy part: *right in the middle* of Israel's repentance ritual, the Philistines roll in with their terrifying army, and "the LORD thundered loudly against the Philistines that day and threw them into such confusion that they were defeated by Israel" (1 Sam. 7:10). The people kept their eyes upon God, trusting His faithful heart to receive them back after so much time betraying Him, and He gave them the victory.

After the battle we see Samuel give the Israelites something beautiful. He provides them—and us—with an invitation to remember what happened in that place. The Israelites, like many of us, so often forget about God's faithfulness toward them. Prone to wander, quick to doubt. Before this moment of victory and many times after it, they utter, "Why, God?" They throw up questions to God with undercurrents of doubt, wondering if God is actually for them or good enough for them.

I understand, though. It's easy to forget when we innately feel forgotten. When remembering goodness is clouded by the hard conditions of life.

So, what does Samuel use to help them remember?

> And the men of Israel went out of Mizpah and
> pursued the Philistines and struck them down
> as far as below Beth-car. **Then Samuel took
> a stone** and set it between Mizpah and Shen,
> and named it **Ebenezer,** saying, **"Thus far
> the LORD has helped us."** So the Philistines
> were subdued and they did not come anymore

within the border of Israel. And the hand of
the LORD was against the Philistines all the
days of Samuel. (1 Sam. 7:11–13, NASB1977,
emphasis added)

God had remembered them. And through an Ebenezer
stone, He gave them a way to remember Him—to remember
that at this very place, when all seemed lost, He helped them.

See, *Ebenezer* means "stone of help." And by erecting it in
front of the people, Samuel invites his people to the simple yet
powerful choice of remembering. From then on, every time
an Israelite saw the stone set up by Samuel, he would have a
tangible reminder of the Lord's power and protection. Said
another way, when the people looked upon the stone, they'd
remember the God who remembered them. This Ebenezer
stone would mark the place God was working, even when it
seemed like all hope was lost. Even when rampant idolatry
was in their past and an army charging them was their future.
Even there. This "stone of help" marked the spot where the
enemy had been routed and also where God's promise to bless
His repentant people had been honored.

An Ebenezer stone says, "This is the place God remembered me. At this point, the Lord helped me. He was here.
Even when I thought He couldn't be."

Our friend Samuel offers us a suggestion. Mark the places
God has worked in your life. Choose to remember them as the
places where God met you, where He was present, even when
you once thought He wasn't. Make a memorial to the goodness and activity of God, an Ebenezer stone. Chart your story

with them, stone by stone, so you can lift your eyes to the work of God in your life in the moments you feel clouded.

Chart Your Ebenezers—Mark Your Story

It's essential to see what we've been saved from so that we can honestly remember what God has done for us. The Lord helped Israel all the way to their first Ebenezer stone. And He will do the same for you. He already has.

Our lives are tiny stones, some half-cracked, some whole, building up a beautiful story of what only God could do. Our stories are full of landmarks, full of moments where God was working, where He showed up in big and small ways.

God remembered Hannah. God remembered her son, Samuel. God remembered His people in battle. They all have moments in their story that, though they couldn't have known it in the moment, they later looked back and realized: God's heart was trustworthy, and His hand was working, even there. Even there on that terribly painful day in the temple. Even there in those dark years where idols lurked. Even there on that battlefield when the Philistines were closing in and the odds looked horrible.

And you know what? God remembers us. *His hand is working.* Even in the parts of our story we think are darkest, and even when we couldn't trace it till now. There's a Bible full of truth and an empty tomb that tells us this. That even in the lowest valleys, He wasn't holding out on His faithfulness. He wasn't withholding hope. Along the way, God has given us glimmers of Himself, signposts that shine an unusually inviting light in what seems overwhelmingly dark and hopeless.

Those signposts, those Ebenezer stones, are *all throughout your journey,* friend. You may not have been able to trace exactly what God was doing at each mile marker, but they are there, bearing witness to the fact that God has helped you up till now. And my hope, by the end of this book, is that you'll be able to tell your own Ebenezer story of how God's heart has been *for* you and His presence has been *with* you in the places you once thought His hand was not at work.

We will walk through each of the "stones" together—places we will stop and consider how God's heart was for us and His hand was moving, even when we couldn't see it at the time. We will raise our Ebenezers together, all the way through. Stone by stone, we'll chart out the places in the path that heaven helped us.

Which means, of course, that we have to start at the beginning. After all, every journey has a starting place—the first mile marker or landmark, if you will. That's your starting stone. It's the first Ebenezer you get to raise, and when you lift your eyes to it, you'll remember the goodness of God again, just like His people did in Samuel's day.

■ ■ ■

As you already know, my starting stone takes the form of those little notes. Such unlikely stones of remembrance, pointing me to hope, love, and safety. They are a gift to look back on. They are evidence that even back then God was stirring my heart to know Him and reach out to Him. Even when I couldn't see things clearly, those little notes reminded me that He was orchestrating a rescue plan for my soul.

Even though childlike in a sense, these notes helped me create a soul rhythm that taught me to look at both the hard and the good. God used them to create an early habit in me that would one day blossom into the ability to hold onto hope even when looking at defeat—remembering His grace in the face of my dismay. As I look back, I see they were little seeds, holding lessons that would fully blossom as God came closer and closer, teaching me things over the long haul. At the time, many of those notes felt like ashes, holding evidence of only pain. And your starting stone may look like ash too, but it's ashes that we rise from. It's ashes that God uses to create something beautiful (Isa. 61:3).

The way hope and light had met me at my starting stone wasn't some coincidence—it was Christ. Jesus was there, pressing into a little girl's heart, carrying her, giving inklings of hope in what seemed so hopeless, holding her hand and guiding her heart. Even on ripped-up pieces of paper, He was teaching me, ever so slowly, how to turn my gaze upward. He was creating something on the inside of me that, now looking back, was a miracle in and of itself. He was giving me, even in those early years, a supernatural endurance to keep me going—even when my heart and mind told me to give up. Even when I couldn't see that He was helping me all along.

We might miss God's grace, but grace does not miss us. We might think we were alone at our starting stone, but we weren't.

Jesus was there.

He was beginning something in us. He was creating the start of something we couldn't see yet.

And like we explored before, it can be really hard to remember He was at work back there, in that early, hard place. It can be hard to remember that the Father's arms make room for all of what our lives, past and present, bring. He holds space for the incidents unseen to others and makes way for healing in them. He knows it is hard for us to remember who He really is when our faith is tired, when our eyes can't see, and when all we want to do is ask why—and so He gives us a way to remember. He builds stones on the journey for us to look back on—evidences of His grace at work. He reminds us, stone by stone, that He was there all along, that hope is always leading us, even when we can't see it.

See, *looking forward,* we can't trace His hand. We have to trust His heart, step-by-step. Much of my story is that—learning to trust His heart when I couldn't trace His hand. And as you read this book, I hope that you'll trust His heart moving forward, too. Especially when you can't see His hand.

But *looking back,* now, *that's* where we can trace things, if we only take the time to lift our eyes. See, God builds the stones. That's His job—to show up in the hard (and good) places of our story and help us along. Our job is to raise those stones up—to acknowledge them and lift our eyes to them and remember that *God helped us in this place. He was here.*

Our job is to keep our eyes up.

And so I wonder: *As you lift your eyes, what is your first Ebenezer? How did God begin your journey with Him? If you could flag the first landmark in the journey—a starting stone— what would yours be?* I don't know how hard your start was with God. I don't know if you were seven or seventeen or seventy-two. I know this: there's an answer to "God, where were You?" He was there. All the way at the start. So I'll ask it again: What is your starting stone?

It may not be notes for you. It may be memories logged in the time capsule of your mind. Maybe all you have to remember is the kindness of someone along the way that pointed you to goodness and hope, which began your quest toward God. Or maybe you remember some sort of overtly spiritual memory that supercharged your Christian journey. Either way, your starting stone is worthy of being remembered. Your *life* is worthy of being remembered. The moments of unseen hurt and pain—and joy too—it's all worth remembering because God has helped you along the way. He really has. Those stories and moments matter; they are markers for us to look back on.

Because just like Samuel told us early on, lest we forget—God has brought us this far.

So, friend, raise your starting stone. Lift your eyes and see it for what it is—the first place grace met you, even when you didn't have eyes to see it at the time.

EYES UP

Lift your eyes and look back on your own journey, taking the time to chart this crucial moment (or season) in your life.

1. Where and when did God build your starting stone?

2. At what point in your story can you sense that God, if ever so faintly, was working to open your heart toward Him?

3. Can you remember the season when you first started thinking about spiritual things? What were those thoughts like? What amazed you or concerned you? What questions did you have? If you prayed, what did you pray about?

4. How did this moment in your story pave the way for you to come to the knowledge of God?

2 | The Stone of Knowledge

Do I Know You?

I've assumed some pretty awful things about people. Saying that out loud stings, but it's true. It humbles the soul when you're reminded of your own iniquity, sin, and endless need for grace.

I've also been on the receiving end and subject to some pretty awful assumptions. I imagine you have too.

> *She's such a shy, reserved introvert. I bet she never initiates conversations with other people to see how they are doing.*

> *She's such a loud, expressive extrovert. I bet she only cares about getting attention.*

> *She's so calculated and analytical. I bet she never takes risks for God or walks by faith.*

She's so spontaneous and free-spirited. I bet she's
irresponsible, never thinking things through.

She's too permissive in her parenting. Her kids
will never understand boundaries.

She's too strict in that household. They're going
to have a complex later on.

The list goes on and on. It's so hard when your character
is put to trial and your intentions are questioned, isn't it? Most
of the time, it hurts the worst when the people who make
these assumptions are supposed to be family—you know, the
trustworthy people in life, the ones you bring in near, the ones
who have heard and seen your heart.

Assumption: "a thing that is accepted as true or as certain
to happen, without proof." I'm not sure why it's so hard for us
to believe that people who are closest to us can make terrible
assumptions. And yet sometimes they do it without blinking
an eye, without trying to come in close and listen, without
pulling up a chair and trying to get to know our heart, without
proof.

If you endure wrong-headed assumptions long enough,
trust always ends up feeling both ethereal and dangerous. At
least it has for me. I want to assume the best, but I've learned
to lean toward the worst: the worst-case scenario, the worst-
case outcome, the worst-case betrayal. And if you add trauma
(more on that later) to those annoying cases of wrong-headed
assumptions, trusting anyone (much less God) eventually
started to feel like a reckless game of Russian roulette, each

time waiting for the shoe to drop, for my heart to be shattered with betrayal, with abandonment, with pain.

I wonder what you do in response to those who assume wrongly about you—or even to trauma you've endured. For me, to avoid betrayal, rejection, or pain, I became skilled at detaching emotionally from relationships before anything derailed. I often still wrestle with this today. I can be quite good at building up walls in case a relationship goes south, high enough to protect my heart, low enough to maintain a persona of gentleness and vulnerability. I wanted people to feel safe with me. However, extending myself in the same manner, I'm learning, isn't something I'm always ready to do. From the outside in, you'd have a hard time knowing that life had taken a soft heart and slowly hardened it with every blow that came its way. Having a hard exterior tricks us into believing we can protect ourselves from the inevitable harshness of life.

So if this is what *we* do when people assume wrongly about us, it would make sense to think that God probably does too. It would make sense for God to detach from us and run the other direction after we assume a bunch of terrible things about Him, over and over and over again. It would make sense for Him to ditch us entirely after we've betrayed Him.

But He doesn't do that. Thank God, He doesn't respond to our wrong assumptions the way we would.

Assuming We Know God

What assumptions about God do you have? I've held some hefty ones.

When I first became a believer, I brought with me the experiences of my life—all of them, good and bad—which impacted how I viewed God and His heart for me. There was little to no proof in my mind at the time that He was good or that His hand was ever working in me or around me. Choosing to trust an invisible and seemingly inactive God was like asking me to trust the people who had once made the heartbreaking assumptions about me, leaving my heart torn and wondering if I'd ever been ready or willing to trust again. The betrayals and abuses from my childhood had embedded in my heart a fear—a fear that said even though I believed good existed somewhere, I would never be able to see it or experience it.

Looking back, I can now see that I was letting my past experiences define who God was. Though I hate it when the assumptions of others call *my* character into question, I was doing that very thing to God. I was letting my circumstances, feelings, and assumptions put Him on trial.

> *I don't feel any warmth or nearness. I bet He's a distant God who likes to stand far away.*

> *There's not an ounce of comfort in this whole situation. I bet He's cold and careless.*

> *I don't see the miracles rolling in. I bet He's inactive. Or angry.*

> *Well, I guess I can see Him doing a few good things for other people. Maybe He is up to some good stuff in this world, but He's not good to me.*

See, I had journeyed past my starting stone. God had worked the beginnings into my story back when I was that little girl with ripped-up notes, drawing me to Him. But I was now at a point in the journey where I needed more. I didn't just need a little-girl *heart* that was slowly warming up to the idea of God in general; I needed a *head* informed on who this God really is. Is He like my assumptions said? Or is He different? I knew enough about Christianity to know I was supposed to trust God, but *who is He*?

Through the Fog to the Stone of Knowledge

With all sorts of pain in our background, getting to know God can seem like an impossible task. Sometimes it feels safer to know *of* Him rather than actually knowing Him. Other times we want to know Him on a deep and intimate level, but circumstances and assumptions and past wounds can tend to make the road foggy in our spiritual journey as we move toward Him—a fog that can get so thick, it's hard to see.

I say that because, let me tell you, I know what fog feels like.

Years ago, Mario and I headed to the mountains to celebrate our one-year anniversary, and more so the fact that we had survived it. I say survival because that's what it was. Twenty-year-old Alexandra and twenty-four-year-old Mario were just happy to have made it a whole year through the undeniable odds that were stacked against us. We'd resolved early on to pave a new way for our family, for ourselves. I knew that coming in we'd have work to do—healing, growing, and tending to were in order.

Apart from celebrating our first year, we were also celebrating our first time away together as a couple. Because of the season of life we had been in, a traditional honeymoon wasn't in the cards for us. We booked a weekend getaway in a most charming town called Sapphire Valley. A sweet older couple with grandkids at the school I worked at had graciously offered it to us for a few days at half the price. And so we jumped at the idea of the two of us celebrating a problematic year that should have broken us. It was also January, which hopefully meant snow and what I hoped was a winter wonderland.

On our way up to the mountain in a tiny Nissan Sentra that was most definitely not equipped for mountain driving, we were prepared to go slow and use extra caution because of the weather. As we went up the mountain, we caught sight of the most beautiful, picturesque views.

"Pull over, Mario! I need to take some photos. I want to remember this forever!" Enjoying waterfalls, creeks, and all that God had to offer up as a masterpiece, I took a deep breath. *This is a new season*, I thought. I could feel it. It was a nice and needed change of pace and scenery compared to the hustle and chaos we consistently took part in.

As we got higher up the mountain, the roads became narrower, and we experienced thick and dangerous fog. Mario's an experienced driver, and so I wasn't afraid—not wholly free of angst but safe. At one point, the fog was so incredibly thick that you could put your hand out the window and watch it disappear into a cloud of white. Our car's high-beam setting was even having a hard time breaking through it. The fear I was experiencing wasn't because of the fog itself but in *what we couldn't see through it*. I was terrified of what was on the other side, and the unknown danger that it potentially held. I assumed every single terrible thing that could've happened like a wild animal running in front of us and ultimately running us off the narrow road, pushing us over the mountain and into boulders. Remember, an assumption is believing something so much so with no proof at all of what we're saying—often driven by fear. I assumed the worst, as I am wildly good at doing.

I think I held my breath the entire drive up.

As we made our way to the level ground, we soon approached a tiny town. The fog began to lift. It was a gradual lifting. About every ten minutes, we'd see it thin as the road ahead became more evident—deep breaths. We could, little by little, see better what was really there in the midst of all that fog—a solid road beneath us and welcoming faces all around us—and the assumptions of what could happen began to fall to the wayside.

You know what that experience taught me? That when we start to see things as they really are, what we thought we knew has no room to stay. That goes for adventurous trips up a mountainside, and it goes for God, too.

So the question becomes this: When life and pain and past experiences create a heavy fog, how do we see God for what's really true about Him? How do we get to the point where we can lay down our assumptions, and even our doubt, to give God (and who He is really is) enough room for discussion? How do we come to a *real* knowledge of His character instead of just relying on our assumptions or circumstances to tell us? How do we move on from our starting stone, keeping our eyes up, so that we might see the next one in our path—the stone of knowledge?

There are lots of answers to that question, but I've found that as we get to know God the Father for who He is *through His Word and His People*—not through the assumptions we've made of Him based on our circumstances—the spiritual fog we find ourselves in begins to lift. Gradually, but it lifts.

God's Word and God's people—that's how we can make out, if even through the fog, who God is. (Well, we also get to know Him through His Son, but we'll get to Him in a bit, I promise.) As I've drawn closer to those two things, I've noticed that I'm communing more with God, sitting with Him more, and really knowing Him as I go.

God's Word

Think back to those people who have assumed wrong things about you. I'm sure we all wish that in those moments we could say something like, "Listen, I know you *think* this or that about me, but I'm looking you in the eyes, and I'm *telling* you otherwise. Instead of leaving my character to your imagination, take me at my *word*. I'm saying, right now, that's not who I am."

Scripture is God's Word—it's God using His words to set straight what we might *think* we know. It gives us the opportunity to *take God at His word* when it comes to His character instead of leaving it up to what someone else says about Him, what someone else has done to us, or even up to our own imagination.

So, what does God say about Himself in His Word? Scripture tells us that God is omniscient (all-knowing), omnipotent (all-powerful), and omnibenevolent (supremely good). In other words, God knows everything, has the power to do anything, and is entirely and perfectly all good.

And that's not all. Scripture also says:

> God is compassionate.
>
> God is gracious.
>
> God is slow to anger.
>
> God is loyal in His love.
>
> God is faithful.
>
> God is Creator.
>
> God is holy.
>
> God is love.
>
> God is relational.
>
> God keeps His promises.
>
> God keeps meeting us.
>
> God tells the truth.
>
> God is driven by love to know us and for us to know Him.

I could keep going here, but stop and consider: Which of those truths is a balm to your soul? Balm for my soul has been remembering that it's not the anger of God that leads Him to give grace but His love. Sweet truth to my ears is the reminder that the God who erected our starting stone in our journey with Him will build every stone on the journey after that so that we can look up and remember He has met us every step of the way, *even when we were in the fog*—even if we're still in it now.

Scripture reveals so much about God. It shows us that He's a God who calls us by name. A God who saw fit to make a way for our redemption, even when we were far from Him and doubting Him and frustrated with Him. A God who forged our union with Christ (more on Him later!). A God who chose to break the veil that once came between us so that we may no longer be separate from His presence. A God who called His creation good and set out on a mission to save us, bring us near, and know Him. A God whose kindness and help aren't based on our doing but on His perfect and holy nature.

Want to take God at His word? His Word says He's always wanted to know you, love you, and bring about a new family for you to belong to—His family. The church. Which brings us to the next way we can, ever so slightly and even through the fog, make out who God really is.

God's People

About ten years ago, I remember the scales falling from my eyes and the fog lifting from my mind when God, through His Word, began to chip away at the hardened heart that left me wondering if God was good or good to me. The fear that once fogged my faith lifted. He was removing my assumptions and undoing years' worth of lies built on years of confusion.

But you know how else He built this stone of knowledge in my life? Through not just His *words* in Scripture but also His *hands and feet* in the world. What do I mean? I mean His people, whom He calls His body (1 Cor. 12; Rom. 12:3–8). It wasn't just chapter after chapter of Scripture but conversation after conversation with those who knew Him, grace by grace, moment by moment, that what I thought I knew about God was replaced with experiencing how much I was known and loved by God. I saw Him through certain people. I experienced the shattering of the walls, word by word, grace by grace, love by love. What I once thought was an angry God was coming into focus now: a loving Father. Through these sweet saints, He tore down my assumptions and my walls. Once held up by my own knowledge, each wall was replaced with the truth about our Holy God. He'd brought me this far again. Leading my soul back to its original Creator, moving mountains so that His daughter would know Him in the way He so beautifully yearns to be in a relationship with us.

I think of people like my mother, whom God used to show me a glimpse of Himself—long-suffering and determined to love. Like my husband, who even amid pain that I so naively inflicted on him, showed me the heart of Christ in forgiveness. Like an employer who so tenderly made way for me at the age of nineteen to wrestle through the Scriptures with her. God chipped away at what I knew, through His hands and feet, and led me to who He is.

Remember Samuel from the Ebenezer stone story? He experienced the same. His name means "heard of God." Samuel had first heard of God thanks to his mother's faithful witness and devotion to God. She'd given Samuel the gift to see God in the midst of the mundane, in the everydayness of their lives. This grace is the gift of seeds being sown in our lives by those around us who have had eyes to see God's hand and also trust His heart. Someone who knows God and has a relationship with God leaves an aroma for us to want to know God, too.

And that shouldn't surprise us, given Ephesians 3:10: "His intent was that now, through the church, the manifold [multifaceted] wisdom of God should be made known to the rulers and authorities in the heavenly realms" (NIV). Did you catch that? The church, God's people, shows the multifaceted wisdom and nature of God. Each member of the body reflects another facet of who God is—helping everyone on heaven and on earth understand His character in all its glory. *The church paints of a picture of what God is like to the watching world.* Each of those people in my life showed me another little angle on who God is, filling in my knowledge of Him, little by little. And the same goes for you. The church members you know, the believers you are in community with—they are part of how God shows you who He is. *What a kindness to us when the fog gets thick,* am I right?

I wonder, *Where has God shown up for you in His Word? Where has He met you through His people?* Taken together, these things help you know God—who He really is. Through them (and through Christ, whom we will get to know later!), He has erected a stone in your story you can always look up to. He has taken you beyond just your beginnings and past your assumptions, into real knowledge of Him. In this second stone of your journey, you can say it with full assurance along with me and all other believers: *He has shown up for me, helping me know Him, even here.*

If you could retrace your steps, where did God build your stone of knowledge? Where did He first introduce you at a deeper level to His Word and His people? Look up to that next Ebenezer stone, friend. Chart it. Mark it. This is how God reveals Himself, and so if you have even the slightest memory of a passage or a person that whispered His character to you, that means *He was meeting you there.*

What's the Point?

It could be easy for us to close this chapter right here. But I can't let you go without making the "so what?" clear to you. Because here's the thing: you could dive into the Scriptures and make a great, and very true, list of God's characteristics. And you could examine all your Christian friends and make a pretty good list of things they teach you about His character, too. And then at the end of that, you might come to the mistaken conclusion that the whole point was to get a list of facts about who God is.

But that's not the point.

The gift of the knowledge of God is more than getting the list right. The true gift of all that knowledge is a *relationship* formed from *yada*, the Hebrew word for "a closeness and nearness."

In Genesis 4:1 (ESV), we see *yada*, when the Bible says Adam intimately "knew" Eve. To know was to experience the other on the most intimate level. We see it again in Genesis 18:19, when God says of Abraham, "I have chosen him so that he will command his children and his house after him to keep the way of the LORD." "Chosen" there is *yada*, to *know*. God *knew* Abraham personally and intimately. This matters for the soul looking for hope in the things that seem so hopeless. Yes, Abraham was chosen and set apart to bring about a new family of many nations, a signpost for King Jesus, for us, for you. And the way Abraham was going to fulfill that purpose was through deeply and relationally *knowing* God in a close, felt way.

As these verses teach us, knowing God isn't informational. It's transformational. When we say we "know God," we're saying He knows us. To *yada* is not merely to know right things about God or His being—though that's important. It's to know His heart so intimately that the very essence of our breath becomes His.

This isn't hard for us to grasp when we really think about it. What makes you trust a person? Consistent experiences of their closeness and nearness to you. In marriage, for instance, I probably wouldn't trust my husband very much if the only form of "knowing" him was returning to some facts about him on a piece of paper. The facts might be true, sure, but I trust him because I've experienced relational closeness with him. He's embodied those character traits in real life—I've witnessed them up close. I don't just know *about* him. I *know* him.

This is true in our friendships too. Whom do you feel like you know best in your life? The people who have drawn close and wrapped their arm around your shoulder during a dark season, I'd imagine. The people who came close when everyone else stood far away. You might have a certain level of knowledge about plenty of people in your life—you know what car they drive, what color their hair is, what they do for a living. But the people who come close? The people who show up and see the real you? The ones who experience the journey *with* you? That's a whole different kind of knowledge.

God doesn't just want you to know about Him. He created you to know—*yada*—Him. Know and experience Him. To have a holy encounter. Up close. In real life. In the dark stretches. And just like it is with our husbands or friends, knowing God in the *yada* way makes room for our hearts to trust God. It makes room in our hearts to say, *"You've brought me this far, Lord."*

And it works the other way around too. He wants to *yada* you. He wants to walk with you through all of your cracks and crevices of life. He wants to experience all the details of your day right alongside you, even in the mundane. He wants to know the questions and the tensions going on inside, no matter how big or scary. And as we let Him do this—let Him in—we realize there's no place He won't go with us. We realize that *to know God is not to be alone in any season of life.*

> *Knowing God in our trauma.*
>
> *Knowing God in our disillusion.*
>
> *Knowing God in our confusion.*
>
> *Knowing God in our pain.*
>
> *Knowing God in our failures.*
>
> *Knowing God in our defeat.*

Experiencing God in this kind of deep, felt, covenant relationship—in both the broken and the healed places—lifts the thick fog from our downcast soul. Knowing, *yada,* that He is the uncreated Creator, who deeply cares. Even when we lack the care to know Him, He wants to know us. *He wants to know you,* friend.

Consider other passages like these:

> "I am the LORD, and I will bring you out from under the yoke of the Egyptians. I will free you from being slaves to them, and I will redeem you with an outstretched arm and with mighty acts of judgment. I will take you as my own people, and I will be your God. Then you will **know** that I am the LORD your God, who brought you out from under the yoke of the Egyptians." (Exod. 6:6–7 NIV, emphasis added)

> And I pray that you, being rooted and established in love, may have power, together with all the Lord's holy people, to grasp how wide and long and high and deep is the love of Christ, and to **know** this love that surpasses knowledge—that you may be filled to the measure of all the fullness of God. (Eph. 3:17–19 NIV, emphasis added)

> I want to **know** Christ—yes, to know the power of his resurrection and participation in his sufferings, becoming like him in his death,

and so, somehow, attaining to the resurrection from the dead. (Phil. 3:10–11 NIV,emphasis added)

We know also that the Son of God has come and has given us understanding, so that we may **know** him who is true. And we are in him who is true by being in his Son Jesus Christ. He is the true God and eternal life. (1 John 5:20 NIV, emphasis added)

This is eternal life: that they may **know** you, the only true God, and the one you have sent—Jesus Christ. (John 17:3, emphasis added)

Do you see how "knowing" is so much more than obtaining the right facts? It's about a real relationship with God—where His characteristics aren't just on a piece of paper; they come to life. They become things you can identify working themselves out in your real life. You can point to the places where He's redeemed you from past slavery, where you've been filled with His love in an unexplainable way, where your suffering feels like you're suffering *with* Him, where you can sense that, as you trust Him with issue after issue, you're getting to know the God who is true to you no matter what.

This is our hope—that our God has always wanted a relationship, not a transaction. To know Him, not just know about Him. More than that, to know Him for who He is, not who we thought He is. And in every single one of our stories, He's made this possible. Somehow, some way, His Word and

His people have found us (or His Son, whom we will explore later) so that we might experience *yada,* a real, deep, and felt knowledge of God. And you want to know what's more? *Knowing God this way propels us to who we are in Him.* As we walk with Him in *yada* knowledge, where we once saw ourselves as forgotten, overlooked, and abandoned, we now see something totally different. Loved. Seen. Valued. Fought for. Known. Amazing how it works, right? True knowledge of God gives us true knowledge of self.

Looking Up

Sister, past experiences can shape us, what we know, and the way we see and move through the journey of life, but they cannot define us. And they can't define God. We don't need them to. Because God has already revealed Himself to us, dear friend. May we have eyes to see and ears to hear, and a heart that knows, *yada,* the Father's love. May we not lean on our assumptions but look to the place in our story where He built the stone of knowledge so that we might see Him for who He is. May we trace the places His Word and His people taught us of His heart. And as we do this, may the fog lift little by little, giving us the space to say, *"Ebenezer. You've brought me this far, Lord."*

Eyes up, friend. Look at your journey. When did He build this stone for you? Chart it. For when you do, you'll be reminded of God's goodness and how far He's brought you. You'll be able to see, maybe for the first time, that even when you thought He wasn't there, *He was.* He may not have shown up the exact way you wanted Him to, but He *was* reaching out through His Word and His people. His heart was to know you and for you to know Him. And He made holy moves to accomplish that.

EYES UP

Lift your eyes and look back on your own journey, taking the time to chart this crucial moment (or season) in your life.

1. Where and when did God build your "stone of knowledge"? (Where in your journey do you see evidence of Him reaching out to you through His Word and His people, so that you might know Him for who He truly is?) What assumptions about God did this tear down?

2. If you had a leaning, have you learned about God's character mostly through His Word or more through His people? Why?

3. What passages of Scripture have most informed you about God's character? What people, in particular, showed you a facet of what God is like?

4. If you feel like you're lacking in your knowledge of God, what steps can you take toward His Word and His people?

5. Why is it important to know that biblical knowledge of God is not just factual but relational?

3 | The Living Stone

Where All the Ebenezers Were Leading

W e're late for school again.
    "It's not her fault."
My mom is talking to the school secretary. She was slightly annoyed with us. I have my ideas as to why. We'll call them assumptions, maybe even some unchecked biases. But I don't know for sure. I just remember her body language, and it was enough for me to feel small and insignificant. This wasn't typical behavior for us, being late to school. But this week, well—this week was the week we'd been thrown into another whirlwind of agony. We'd been kicked out of our house by my biological father. We pulled into our drive to find our clothes lying out in the front yard and a car I didn't recognize parked in our driveway.
    "Who is that, mom?"
    "That's your brother and his mom."

I didn't know I had a nine-year-old brother. I didn't know he lived in our city and that on that day, he would be moving into the place I'd learned to call home.

I was eight years old and in the second grade. It was the same year I had an angel of a second-grade teacher who encouraged me to write and use my words as love and light. It was the same year I was awakened to the stark reality that our life was not like the lives of my friends. I wasn't aware of the dysfunction until I noticed how others around us reacted to our circumstances. I felt the shame of the old car we had to drive, the sting of our broken household, and the compassion for a single mother who knew little English.

The secretary is giving my mom an earful.

"If Alexandra's having a hard time getting up in the mornings, you need to make sure she's being disciplined for it. She needs more structure. Is she going to bed on time? She's been late three days in a row now."

My mom sighs. She's late to work now, too. I can only imagine what my mom must have been feeling. How could she even begin to explain the trauma and pain we had been experiencing? How could she tell her that we were now sleeping in a friend's borrowed basement in a totally different part of town, which forced us to wake up and drive an hour to school? How could she say any of this without falling apart, without the grief and hurt overtaking her?

She kept a brave face on for me and took the blows that came our way, as many as she could humanly bear. She safeguarded my heart with whatever grit she had left. The stings rendered her silent. She couldn't find the words to paint a picture. She couldn't string together anything other than, "It's not her fault. I'll try to get here on time tomorrow."

At that moment, all we had was love, and grit, and a desire to keep on. And for my mom, her one desire to give me a chance at life—at a new life—was her drive and reason. So much like the posture and resolve of Jesus.

In that moment with my mom, I experienced a level of sacrificial love I hadn't ever known before. I'm sure she took hits for me before then, of course. Before we stood there with that secretary, there was a whole history behind us—a series of unfortunate events, where people chose themselves over honor and love, with moments of profound selfishness and greed, where lust and gluttony got the best of them, leaving a trail of sin and suffering. Yes, she had endured those things well before now. But this moment in the school office—this is the one I remember landing in my heart differently from others. This is the one that registered. The one that meant something.

It's not her fault. In those words, I could tell she reflexively felt my pain right along with me. I could feel her taking the blow for my transgression of tardiness and the shame associated with it, all so I wouldn't have to. I could feel her taking my place and shielding me from my accuser. And that? It changes a person.

Where the Stones Were Leading

Have you ever had anyone take a hit for you? Have you had someone carry the weight that was not theirs to carry? Have you had someone love you so much they'd rather take the consequences of the hard in turn for your good?

I can promise you the answer to these questions is yes, no matter what your story is. You may or may not have memories of a family member or friend doing this for you, but the answer is still yes. You know why? Because there's One who has most definitely done this for you. His name is Jesus Christ. And His version of taking a hit for you is better than anyone else's.

So, who is Jesus Christ really? He's the One who, through His life, death, and resurrection, changed everything for us. He's the point in our story where God didn't just show up in part *but in full*. He's where all our little Ebenezer stones were leading. Remember your starting stone? The place God started to warm your heart toward Him in small ways? Your heavenly Father built that Ebenezer moment in your journey to lead you to Jesus. Your stones of knowledge, remember them? Those seasons when God built your knowledge of who He is through His Word and His people? Those mile markers in your journey were also fashioned by the Father's hand to keep you on the path that leads to Christ! This stone, friend. It's the one all the others made their way toward.

But let's pause for a moment. When you hear Jesus's work of "life, death, and resurrection," do those sound like big, churchy, theological words? Do your eyes gloss over a little bit when we talk about how Jesus is "the way God shows up for us in full"? For a long time in my life the answer to these questions was *yes* and *yes*! So let's slow down and explore what all this stuff means for us. Because friend, *this Ebenezer moment in your story—the one where you really met Jesus and trusted Him for who He truly is—is the greatest stone God has built in your story.*

I know the path through life can be exhausting at times, and it's hard to see God's hand moving at certain points—especially those rough patches and those long stretches that feel like you're in a deep, dark wood. But you can't miss this point in the journey. This stone is the Ebenezer of all Ebenezers; it's the one the others were building up to; *it's the ultimate proof God really has shown up for you and for me.* It's the evidence we crave when we shake our fist at heaven and wonder where in the world God is. It's the answer we can slam our other fist down on the map of our life, in confidence, saying, "There. He showed up for me in the fullest way *right there.*"

This stone, friend. Let's learn all we can about it and then lift our eyes to it together. Now, the Bible has a lot to say about Jesus and how we come to meet Him in our journeys. But since we only have one chapter to think through this, let's just go with five things we can bank on.

Jesus, the Way We See God

We can see God in a lot of ways, as we saw in previous chapters. But sometimes we miss the places God reveals Himself most. We turn our heads one direction, toward some circumstance we are fixated on, and stare at it, screaming up to heaven, "Reveal Yourself here! Where are You?" And we saw in the last chapter that God isn't silent in that moment. He actually has an answer to that. His response is something to the tune of "Beloved, I *have* revealed Myself, but on My terms. Turn your head over here, in this direction, and look. See how I've revealed Myself in My Word and My people? See those places I was meeting you through the hands and feet of My body? See how I directed you and comforted you and shepherded you through My Word in moments you really needed it? See how I filled in the details of who I am in the Scriptures so you can hold on to what's true, even in the dark? Dear one, I *have* shown up. I *have* revealed Myself. But you must turn your head and look to the places I choose to reveal Myself most. Here, let Me give you eyes to see."

Having the eyes to see where God is actually revealing Himself. Isn't that the hardest thing in the world to do? In so many moments of my life, the answer is yes. But when I stumble across certain Bible characters, I find I'm not alone.

I can relate a whole lot to our friend Phillip, for example, a disciple of Jesus who spent many of his days being in the presence of the Messiah but not fully believing or maybe even understanding His power. Do you remember how he questioned Jesus in John 14:8?

> "Lord," said Philip, "show us the Father, and
> that's enough for us."

"Show us the Father." Tell me that isn't the cry of your heart sometimes! *Show me. Show up for me. Reveal Yourself here, for the love! And it will finally be enough for me.*

How does Jesus respond?

> Jesus said to him, "Have I been among you
> all this time and you do not know me, Philip?
> The one who has seen me has seen the Father.
> How can you say, 'Show us the Father'? Don't
> you believe that I am in the Father and the
> Father is in me? The words I speak to you I do

not speak on my own. The Father who lives
in me does his works. Believe me that I am
in the Father and the Father is in me." (John
14:9–11)

Who knows what it is exactly, but Philip clearly has some
sort of expectation in his head when it comes to how God
should reveal Himself. Or perhaps, as I tend to think, he was
carrying around a deep sense of doubt about who, in fact, God
is. Either way, Philip has fully functioning vision and still can't
see God showing up for him, *in the flesh, right before his very
eyes,* in the person of Jesus Christ. He is missing the work of
Christ right in front of Him! He has some other scenario in
mind, some other way He thinks God should be shown to
him, but thankfully Jesus doesn't leave him in that place. To
free him, Jesus gently reminds Philip of the truth. He lovingly
corrects Philip's assumptions about how God chooses to reveal
Himself and helps him see that He, in fact, was the very One
Phillip was still looking for.

Jesus tells him the truth:

> *Philip, I am the way the Father reveals Himself.
> I—Me, this man in front of you—is how you
> can see God. God shows up in many ways, but
> I'm the fullest way. God has worked through His
> Word and His people to show Himself to you,
> but He wanted to come even closer. He wanted
> to show up in flesh and blood. That's why I'm
> here. That's who I am. I'm God, touching down
> to the earth, showing up to the chaos, revealed
> to you in the flesh. You don't have to wonder if*

*God will ever show His face to you in this season
because He's looking at you, dead in the eye,
right now.*

Friend, if you're wondering how God reveals Himself in full form in your life, *it's Jesus.* Yes, we want to see God move in our situations. Yes, we want to see Him work things out for our good. Yes, we want to see Him intervene in our circumstances. And we should pray toward all those things! But here's the truth: *Jesus is ultimately how we see God.* If you're wondering where God is, if you're desperate to know if He's really shown up, the answer is Jesus. Yes, God is right here with you in the chaos. *In Jesus.* Yes, God has really touched down and shown up. *In Jesus.* He is the ultimate place we can point to and say, "God showed up here for me. In a major, jaw-dropping, irreversible way."

Seeing Jesus wasn't enough for Philip because He didn't recognize the face he was looking into. But that doesn't have to be true for you and me. We can look at Jesus and know—this is the face of God. This man is the way God shows up in our lives. This man is the answer to where God's been all along. We can look back on our story and remember the moment we, like Paul, "saw and understood God in the face of Christ" (2 Cor. 4:6 MSG), and *it was enough for us.*

Have we been around Jesus all this time and not seen Him for who He truly is? Have we been around His grace and mercy and perhaps missed it? Have we been looking for some other way for God to meet us and totally missed the reality that He *has* met us in the person of Jesus? Did we miss the whole point of His existence—that is *Jesus* is the truest and biggest way God reveals Himself in our stories? Are we looking for some other miracle, good as it may be to pray for, and yet missed the best one?

Remember friend, when we look at Jesus, we see the kindness of the Father. *We see God Himself.* If you tend to forget this about Christ, find a way to hold up the truth in front of your eyes using verses like these:

> [Jesus] is the image of the invisible God,
> the firstborn over all creation.
> For everything was created by him,
> in heaven and on earth,
> the visible and the invisible,
> whether thrones or dominions
> or rulers or authorities—
> all things have been created through him
> and for him.
> He is before all things,
> and by him all things hold together.
> (Col. 1:15–17)

> Long ago God spoke to our ancestors by the prophets at different times and in different ways. In these last days, he has spoken to us by his Son. God has appointed him heir of all things and made the universe through him. The Son is the radiance of God's glory and the exact expression of his nature, sustaining all things by his powerful word. (Heb. 1:1–3)

You need these reminders. *I* need these reminders. We all need them. Because we all are going to experience so many "Philip moments"—those frustrating days when we want to shout to heaven, "I just can't see You in this! Show me where You are!" In those moments we all need the loving help of Scripture to remind us that—you know what?—we can see God just fine because the way to truly see Him is to look at Christ. So let's take these truths to the bank, shall we? Let's tape them on our dashboards in the car, or write them on our mirrors in the bathroom. Whatever it takes. *Eyes up. God has shown up for you. He has touched down in this crazy world. You can see Him. In Christ.*

Jesus, the One Who Gives You New Eyes to See Grace

As I've mentioned before, a lot of the questions surrounding the goodness and character of God are ones that stem from what we believe about God and how we see God. "God, I don't see You here" is a sentiment we've all shared, along with Philip, at one point or another. But then, at some point, we realize that Jesus shows us who God is. He lets us see God. And in that moment, the scales fall from our eyes, giving us new sight, new vision, and new life. We couldn't see before. But because of Jesus's power to reveal God to us, we have new eyes.

I remember the first time I could see in this way. I remember when I first noticed God's clear hand over my life, even though I couldn't pinpoint it before.

I was twenty-two years old, sitting in a Sunday service listening to the pastor share a message on the grace of God. I don't remember the sermon title, but I do remember one of the verses he was teaching. It was Ephesians 2:4–7:

> But God, who is rich in mercy, because of his great love that he had for us, made us alive with Christ even though we were dead in trespasses. You are saved by **grace**! He also raised us up with him and seated us with him in the heavens in Christ Jesus, so that in the coming ages he might display the immeasurable riches of his **grace** through his kindness to us in Christ Jesus. (emphasis added)

I wrote this down on my church bulletin right away. God gives a certain kind of grace that made all things new, not based on merit but in love. And this grace is a gift that has the power to bring about beauty from ashes, life from death.

I spent many years wrestling with the tension of God's grace and goodness in my life. I would look back at my life and wonder, *Where were you when . . . ? Where was grace in the chaos of my circumstances?* This wasn't an easy question to answer until I began to understand what grace really means. For starters, God's grace flows from the essence of his being: "The LORD, the LORD, a God merciful and gracious, slow to anger, and abounding in steadfast love and faithfulness" (Exod. 34:6 ESV). That's something that isn't just true about Jesus; it's true about God from the start of the Bible to the very end.

In the New Testament, *grace* is translated from a term meaning "divine favor," "goodwill," "that which gives joy," and "that which is a free gift." In other words, grace is the undeserved gift of God, and in its fullest expression, that gift is Christ Jesus.

As I rocked my youngest daughter back and forth in the wooden church pew, I began to see Jesus through a different lens—the lens of grace. In all the flurry of my anxiety to see where grace could possibly be in a hard life like mine, God finally gave me new vision to see—*there He was, the grace of heaven sent straight to me.* He was gently guiding me back to remember His character: God is infinite, eternal, and unchanging in His being, wisdom, power, holiness, justice, goodness, and truth. Grace became the determining factor for my life, and let me tell you: it can be for yours too. It's the gift that reconciles the hard, the ugly, the unforeseeable, and unforgettable, making all things new.

I believe we've missed seeing God in our lives because we've not known what we're looking for. But with new eyes given to us by Jesus, we can learn to spot the moments of grace woven in and through our stories. Jesus opened our eyes to who He truly is, and once we see Him clearly, well, we start seeing evidence of His work all over the place. Now that we have spiritual eyes—whew, friend—grace pops out everywhere, doesn't it? It's like we are suddenly able to catch a glimpse of God's love all around us. We can look back and see the moments He gifted hope to us when we were lost in the dark, damp pit of despair. *Thank You, Jesus, for the grace-gift of faith and the help to hold on!* We can look back and see the times He gave us the strength to keep going when all we wanted to do was give up. *Thank You, Jesus, for the grace-gift of fortitude!* We can look back to the times when we endured discomfort and pain and betrayal and remember the moments

He came near and brought us the grace-gift of comfort from it all. *Thank You, Jesus, for Your nearness and kindness to us in the place of sorrow!*

I could keep going. And I bet you could too. I imagine your story has similarities to mine. Bills paid when there was no money left in the account. Housing situations figured out when we had nowhere to go. New friendships out of nowhere when we were lonely. Fresh courage poured out when we were paralyzed by fear. Where is God? When Jesus gives us new eyes, we can see and say with confidence, *He's everywhere. His handprints are all over my story, and they are holding grace, grace, and more grace.*

That's what Jesus does. He's God in the flesh, and he's also an eye-opener. He is the gift of heaven to you and me, and when we are given the ability to truly see that gift, we can then see a million other gifts sprinkled all over our journey. *God has been there.* We just needed the gift of sight to see His fingerprints—the multitude of graces extended to us over the course of our life. And in Jesus we are given just that.

Jesus, the One Who Gets You

I scrolled past the picture-perfect photo of a woman with her family on Instagram and just about threw my phone. No, I'm serious. I was mindlessly scrolling as I waited to check out at a store in the mall. My kids were exhausted from the day. I double-tapped the picture because I somehow want to prove to myself that just for a second, I was not the bitter woman who couldn't stand to see someone else happy.

How wildly unrelatable, I thought. She doesn't get it.

But was it this women's job to be the space where I found comfort? Did I need to see only the unraveling of someone's life to feel like they could relate to mine? I suppose that, deep down, I wanted to know that others around me were experiencing the same nightmare of a season as I was, the rejection, the marital pain, the lack of clarity and direction in my season of life, the deep sense of unworthiness.

I don't think I was jealous of her life. Rather, I believe the picture evoked the nagging feeling that I most certainly did not have much of anything together. That my efforts to present myself anything other than tidy came up empty. We spend so much of our time looking to relate to and be seen by others, to find understanding and acceptance, to quickly find that no one can ever meet us the way our souls beckon for it, that no amount of empathy can heal the depth of our wounds or fill the void to be understood. And often we rely on the circumstantial temperature of life to help us gauge how our hearts and minds should feel and be. But what if we could find a better thermometer?

Friend, we can. Because here's the deal: where that woman on Instagram can't possibly understand every single thing I'm facing, *Jesus can.* Hear me loud and clear: the problem isn't that you and I want to feel deeply understood on all the levels. It is normal for us to experience that kind of desire. The problem is that we look for this experience in the wrong people and things. Where everyone else won't have the ability to get your pain, or understand you in all your complexity, Jesus will. *He gets you. And He gets the pain you're going through.*

But don't take my word for it. Take the Word of God Himself in Hebrews 4:14–15. In this passage, Jesus is described as our "great high priest" who has the power to take His rightful place in the heavens because He's unique. We already know one way He's unique—we just explored this a few paragraphs ago. Jesus is *God* in the flesh. He's divine. He's the way we see God himself! Only *God* can take God's throne, and because Jesus *is* God, He has the right to sit on the heavenly throne! But don't miss the "in the flesh" part of this equation. There's another way He's unique—He's human, too. Just like you and me. Jesus, God *and* human! Read it for yourself:

> "Therefore, since we have a great high priest who has passed through the heavens—Jesus the Son of God—let us hold fast to our confession. *For we do not have a high priest who is unable to sympathize with our weaknesses, but one who has been tempted in every way as we are, yet without sin.*" (emphasis added)

Because Jesus is not just God, but God in the flesh, He has not only made it possible for God to be understandable to us but also for our daily issues to be physically understandable to Him. In other words, He's relatable. He knows what it's like to be us. He is not only an "up there" or "out there" God. He's also a God who came *here*, who comes close.

Have you ever thought about that? That Jesus knows what it's like to be you in a way no one else does? He knew frustration and weakness. He endured temptation and pain. Not only can we relate to Him, but He can relate to us. Because He became one of us, He is a Savior who gets it. Who gets *you*. And, as a result, we now know Him as a great high priest who is approachable in the moments we need grace and mercy.

When you see Jesus in your mind's eye, what is He like? Does He have a halo on top of His head, with a warm golden glow in the background, holding cute little sheep in His arms as He frolics down a yellow brick road? Because that's not how the Bible actually paints His life here on this earth. Like you and me, He is instead painted as a human with weaknesses, suffering, ailments, and constant assaults from the fall at every turn, wrestling with everything you and I wrestle with. He understands the nuances of life and the layers that come with being an embodied human on this side of heaven.

This is our Jesus. He knew what it was like to seek the Father's help, grace, compassion, mercy, power, and presence desperately and *often*. Yes, He lived a sinless, perfect life that was a sufficient offering to God for our sins, but that does not mean He always had perfect circumstances or that He never experienced the temptations you and I experience. He did not live a life absent of the trials you and are faced with every day. He was tempted in every way, and offered up prayers and appeals to the Father when the ripples of life's waves came crashing down on His heart (Heb. 4:15; 5:7).

Friend, hear this: whatever it is, Jesus gets it. He is with you and for you and came to give you a way forward because He knew what your situation was like and He couldn't bear not to walk through it by your side. Jesus is your God, high and lifted up above you, and He's also your brother—human in the flesh right by your side. *He is both*, and there is no other God like that. The One who's God and the One who gets it. To what better place or person could you possibly lift your eyes?

Jesus, Your Hit Taker

I know. We could just close the chapter right there because, *hallelujah,* Jesus is good. But there's even more.

Yes, Jesus is the One who knows what it is to be high and lifted up as the glorious God that He is. And yes, Jesus is the One who also knows what it is to be humble and brought low as an ordinary human, too. But on top of that, he's also the One who knows what's it's like to be a *hit-taking* human on behalf of other humans. What do I mean? I mean that He didn't just endure the typical blows that come with life in a fallen world. (We all take those on the chin at some point, am I right?) On top of those, He took the blows other people deserved.

When I think back to my mom in that office, I can't help but well up with tears. Because her example gives a living picture of what Jesus does for us all. Accusation and shame headed straight for you and for me, and Jesus stepped in to absorb it all, in our place. *I'll take on whatever her faults deserve.* That's the message of the cross, you know. Some of the blows in this life—you didn't deserve them. That's called suffering. But others, well, you *do* deserve them because you did wrong and you know it. That's called sin. As Romans says, we've all sinned. And sin requires payment—a score settled before God, all our wrongs made right. And the payment for those sins? Death. Blood.

I know, that sounds gruesome. But when you think of how people talk about settling scores, this logic comes out, right? We say things like "He was out for blood," or "Her blood is on your hands" or "They were bloodthirsty." We all know, deep down, that the "wages of sin is death."

God isn't very fair if He doesn't require payment for every wrongdoing, no matter the person or the status, right? And so you and I are in a pretty rough situation because we have a record of sin in our filing cabinet, demanding payment no matter how much we put it off.

The judgment that was rightly reserved for all that sin, it was just waiting for us. The cross was a place you (and I, and all of us) were destined for, metaphorically speaking. And yet we didn't have to go there or suffer there or pay for our wrongs. Jesus hightailed it to the cross so we wouldn't have to, so He could take the hit for us, and so our record could be clean. All that sin, paid for. All the shame associated with it, *gone*. How? Because He was without sin. He was the only one qualified to pay the bill on our behalf.

Isn't that wild? Jesus took the hit in your place, defended you, and then He shielded you. And now He lives to help you. He did all this on your behalf. Because of His work on the cross, He now stands before any accuser and says, "I've already paid the penalty for everything you might point out about her. You cannot cast blame on her any longer. All her debts are paid by me—past, present, and future. What you're hurling at her has no place to land because I've already taken those blows on her behalf. You have no place here."

Friend, are you feeling the place of rest and restitution that Jesus is for you? I know you may have a heart or a life that feels shattered, and I get that. But all our pieces are put back together in the presence of a Savior who says, "Sit with me. I've come to bring new life, living water, and My body broken for you." For He's the only One who has gone to the lengths of *death* to prove His love for you and pay for all the sin and the suffering that has taken a toll on your story.

Plaster this everywhere your eyes might see it: *Jesus's work on the cross shows us that God really is good.* He wouldn't have set up this unfathomable rescue plan, nor would He have taken the hit for us, if He weren't good. The cross reveals God's goodness and character to whole new levels. And through Him, we can intimately know God in the way God wants to be known. Through Him, we understand who God truly is and how far He is willing to go so that we might know Him!

Jesus, Your Living Stone

There are a million more things we could lift our eyes to when it comes to Jesus, but here's the last thing we'll talk about in this chapter—*and it's so good.* It really is the whole climactic point of the story of Jesus.

Here it is: Jesus didn't just go through death on your behalf. He came out on the other side of death, *alive*.

He beat death. Slayed it, right in its tracks.

Take that in.

Jesus died. And then He came back to life. Your Jesus, your God, your Christ defeated the world's biggest enemy. The enemy none of us has any power over in the end. And yet Jesus does.

He went into the grave, and then in the power of the Spirit *He walked out of it.* And He did that to make a way for you and me to do the same thing one day. That's right. When you and I die, we don't just go to heaven forever in the state of a spirit-blob or something. We will die, yes. And then one day *we'll resurrect just like Jesus did*. Because He overcame the enemy of death, we will, too. We'll straight-up *walk out of our grave* and live forever with Him, physically, in a world made totally new and right and amazing and everything it should have been before sin infected it. *That's your future,* friend. Jesus made it so. And that future is secure.

What can we call such a Savior? First Peter 2:4 gives us some good words to choose from, I think. Peter tells us that Jesus is our "living stone." He was rejected as worthless by others, but in God's sight, He was chosen and precious. And notice the stone isn't dead or lifeless. It's the *living* stone. How fitting. We know now why Peter chose to use that word. Because Jesus was resurrected! Jesus is the foundational stone we build our whole lives on, and He's called a living stone because *He's alive*. Right now.

> He can hear your prayers to Him because only living people can hear things, and He's alive.

> He can answer those prayers because, again, He's alive.

> He can intercede for you in heaven right now because He's alive.

> He can pour out grace and mercy in your time of need because He's alive to do it.

Are you feeling this? I mean, think about that—no other figure in all of history can make this claim. They all died at some point and never got out of the grave. But your God?

Your Jesus? He got up and out, and He hears you and moves on your behalf right now because His resurrected heart is beating—beating for His people, for you and for me.

Drink this in: Jesus isn't just your foundational stone in a stale religious sense; He's your *living* stone because life is coursing through His blood and His bones. Where others still lie in their graves, the tomb of your Christ is empty. Looking back at this truth—at the cross and then the empty tomb where our Savior once lay—is the very thing that keeps us when the darkness of the world overshadows the hope we strive to keep.

Looking Up

I want you to know that your life will have pieces in it that will not make sense, where grace feels sparse and life feels empty and your soul flaky, but God is in it. God exists in your pain, happiness, and healing. They can all coexist, and God exists in all of them. Jesus's life was a picture of this, abandoned by most, rejected by many. He carried the good and the bad at the same time and did so with zero sinful responses involved. Our friend, Jesus, carried it all for us and kept on. He kept walking toward the cross, knowing that His way forward would pave the way for our debts to be paid and our future to be secure.

He did all of this so you might have someone to show you the face of God when you thought He was hiding it, someone to open your eyes to grace, someone to really get your world, someone to take the hit for you, and someone to beat your biggest enemy so you might have a path toward new life.

What grace! Grace, this is it, friends. As we see Jesus, we see God and we see love. And His presence and guidance are what carry us from stone to stone in our journeys, from Ebenezer to Ebenezer. Can you see it? Each past stone in your story was leading to this one: the place where you met the living Stone, Jesus Christ. And once we meet Him at that juncture, He then walks with us through every other mile marker along the path afterwards. What I mean to say is that Jesus is the Stone that takes you and me to the next stone, the next season, the next day. As we face what comes, we look to Him and remember that God is still here and God is still good. After all, look what He's done for us in Christ!

I have to ask: Do you know the point in your story where this Ebenezer stone, the living Stone of Jesus, was built? Can you look back and point to the moment you came to know Jesus? Have you met Him, truly? Do see His love yet? Do you see how even now He's contending for you?

If not, *run to Him*. Like Philip, you may not know it, but He's everything you're looking for. Because God sent a Savior for you, on your behalf, knowing the nuance of it all, to take the weight and wrath, the sting of sin and death so that you would have a chance, an option, a path made straight with a way at a new life. He waits to be your living Stone, your living hope. Run to Jesus.

And if you have met your living Stone, Jesus Christ, at some point in your life's journey, mark this moment in your story—the Lord brought you this far. You may be nodding along right now. On the head level, you know Jesus took your place, absorbing the penalty for your transgressions and bearing your shame. But think through your story: When did you not just know this intellectually but experientially? When did you *feel* it, personally, for the first time, sort of like I felt it for the first time with my mom? When did it make a difference or register in a new way? When was your "office moment" with Jesus, where the reality of Him taking blows for you moved from Bible trivia to life changing? When were you introduced for the first time in a way that meant something to you, to the living Stone?

Mark it, chart it, highlight it. However you'll remember it. *This is the moment He showed you who Jesus is,* and no matter how dark the road gets, you can look back at this Ebenezer moment where God lifted your eyes to Christ. This will be the moment of grace that will keep you going when nothing else could. You can say it confidently: *He was right here, meeting me and showing me Himself in the work and the death and resurrection and the face of Jesus. He wouldn't have done that if He weren't good.*

Raise that Ebenezer, right here, right now.

Because you're going to need it for the next stone.

EYES UP

Lift your eyes and look back on your own journey, taking the time to chart this crucial moment (or season) in your life.

1. Has anyone ever "taken a hit" for you? What were the circumstances? How did that make you feel?

2. Where and when in your faith journey did God introduce you to Jesus, the "living stone"? What was that like? Did you face any fears or challenges? Was it an all-at-once experience or a drawn-out one?

3. Of the five things in this chapter that we learned about Jesus, our living Stone, which one was new for you, or stood out in a specific way? Why?

4. What passages of Scripture have most informed you about who Jesus is? How did those passages challenge you, encourage you, or surprise you?

5. Is there anyone in your life who has not hit the "living stone" moment in their journey? How might you help introduce them to Jesus?

4 | The Grieving Stone

A Shepherd in the Darkness

It's May 27, 2019—Memorial Day. Mario and I are corralling the kids to head over to my in-laws for the yearly family gathering. We can't find Sophia's shoes and are already running behind. "Mario, will you text your parents to let them know we're running late?"

They are gracious in their response as always: "Don't worry, daughter, you're good." If you've ever had the pleasure of meeting my in-laws, you'd know what it's like to meet warmth and compassion. They are the people you know have been with God, the ones whose aroma is that of Jesus. They are and were and will be one of my greatest gifts.

We arrived only thirty minutes late. I'm ready to relax—this is what we all needed. *Reprieve*, I think to myself. My mother-in-law has a way of making everyone feel at home, and her food is everything that is southern cooking. The banquet of delights was everything a southern cookout should

be, including my mother in-law's famous baked macaroni and
cheese. (In case you're wondering, the magic that lives inside
of that blessed dish, that would be two pounds of macaroni
noodles, six eggs, whole milk, salt, pepper, a bag of sharp
cheddar cheese, a bag of mild cheddar cheese, a few packs of
butter, and some anointing that can only come from the hands
of someone who has offered this macaroni and cheese up as a
love offering to the Lord.)

I envision what is about to happen. The boys and my
father-in-law would head out to play basketball at a nearby
park as often as possible. It was a rhythm, a tradition of sorts, a
place of peace and connection for them. They talked through
life and learned things that only a sacred basketball game can
offer between a dad and his boys. And this year was no different. Just as I anticipate, they decide to go out for a game after
dinner. Several of us follow behind. The kids, my mother-in-
law, and aunts stay back.

"Are you sure, Mom? Don't you want to come?" I ask my
mother-in-law.

"No, it's okay. I'll stay back with the kids. Y'all go ahead."

It doesn't take us long to get there. The park is just a few
minutes down the road. The boys play game after game, the
sun is out, the energy is high, there's music and laughter. And
then the next minute—there's not.

What happens next changes our lives forever. The unimaginable. As he decides to head back home to rest, my father-in-
law suddenly collapses just a few feet away.

We plead, we cry, we shout, and we sit in shock. It's all a
fog of pain and anguish, a nightmare of hurt. The careless and
free atmosphere in the park comes to an instant halt. You can

feel the fear and sting in the air, taking over. The ambulance pulls up and finds a community of people praying down the heavens, undone by the heartache, bargaining with God for a miracle. We are waiting to hear good news, any news.

I am fully human and fully daughter of God at this moment—angry but also hopeful. Overcome with suffering and looking up to the heavens, reminding myself that there is still a God who has the power to bring us comfort and help right in the middle of harm's way.

My father-in-law is taken to the hospital. My mother-in-law, husband, and brother-in-law follow. Several of us head back to the house. I begin to ready myself—the babies are at home. They may have stayed back with an older cousin, but news travels fast in a community like this. I knew they already knew. I walk back into the house, disoriented, and head upstairs to check on the them as we waited for the news no one could bear to hear.

My two youngest are asleep, but my oldest is wide awake. She's afraid. I am too. She weeps in my arms as I console her. "Hey, let me read something to you, okay?" I reach over to her side table and grab her Discovery Kids Bible and head to Psalm 23. Nothing is well, nothing can prepare you for this sort of suffering—and all I know to do is open the words that have brought reprieve before—where I have found my soul to be well, even in the valley.

I start telling her the truth I've rehearsed for so long in those shadow moments of life. "The Lord is our Shepherd, Leilla. He lets us rest in green meadows and leads us beside peaceful streams."

He renews my strength.
He guides me along right paths, bringing
    honor to his name.
Even when I walk through the darkest valley,
I will not be afraid, for you are close beside
    me.
Your rod and your staff protect and comfort
    me.
You prepare a feast for me in the presence of
    my enemies.
You honor me by anointing my head with
    oil. My cup overflows with blessings.
Surely your goodness and unfailing love will
    pursue me all the days of my life,
and I will live in the house of the LORD for-
    ever. (Ps. 23:3–6 NLT)

"Amen, baby girl?"

"Amen, Mom."

The tears flow. *The Lord is our Shepherd. He's brought us this far.*

Then a distant ring of someone's phone. We get the call. He didn't make it.

The Grieving Stone

Do you like hearing other people's testimonies? The story of how they came to know the Lord? I do. Gosh, I love hearing those stories. They build my faith and help me see the God who can write a million stories at once, all making their way toward His goodness and love. But you know what I notice a lot in people's testimonies? They stop in a place I don't think testimonies are actually supposed to stop. It's like they go along the same journey as we've been in this book—from those early days of being stirred toward God and then coming into deeper knowledge of Him through His Word and His people, and then finally coming to Christ!—and then bam, the story is over. That's the whole testimony. From nonbeliever to finally believer. From the Starting Stone to the Living Stone.

But there are more stones. There's a *whole life* on the other side of coming to Jesus, a whole set of mile markers we have yet to pass, markers we are walking toward. A whole host of hills and valleys. And Jesus wants to walk alongside us through every single one of them. I mean, that's the whole point of coming to the living Stone right? That we might not just meet Christ and call it a day but start *walking* with Him through the rest of the Ebenezer moments ahead.

I wonder what stones exist on the other side of your "living Stone moment," the moment you came to Christ. I imagine that you, like me, can tell the tale of a life that didn't become picture-perfect the day after we became Christians. If anything, for many of us, it seems like right after the living Stone was erected in our lives—a climactic moment where we finally met Jesus—the path started to lower into a valley.

Is that true for you? When I look back on that moment at the park with my father-in-law, I can tell you it's certainly true for me. As I said, I was daughter of God at that moment, full of hope and life. But I was also a citizen of a fallen world that hasn't been made all-the-way right yet, a world that's still full of death and darkness as it waits for Jesus to finally and fully bring His kingdom to earth.

I didn't have the words for it at the time, but this new Ebenezer moment I was facing, this mile marker in my journey—it was a grieving stone. Yet another place I was going to have to trust Jesus to show up. *Would God meet me here? Could He bring me and keep me and carry me here, this far?* It's one of those moments I'd prefer to leave out of my story, but what if God wanted it to be part of my larger testimony?

What if the valley wasn't a section of my story God wanted me to minimize or erase but rather a place He wanted to prove Himself true to me and near to me? What if He wanted me to see that He's a God who is willing to go low, descending into the deep-dark-hard places, in order to stay by my side? What if He wanted to reveal that this place of grief isn't too much for Him and won't scare Him off? What if He wanted to show me yet another place I could trust Him to show up? What if He wanted to give me yet another stone in my journey that I could look back and say, "He has helped me and brought me this far"?

Well. Thankfully I don't have to wonder *what if.* Because the answer was made clear.

The Good Shepherd Who Leads

After that phone call, the news spreads like wildfire to the family.

My father-in-law. He's gone.

It's hard to even try to piece together the moments that follow, but I somehow make it to the hospital, back to a room where I find my husband, mother-in-law, and a few others weeping. The pain is indescribable.

God be near. God be here.

My mother-in-law asks me to pray, an unimaginable ask amid the anguish. There are three pastors in the room, much more equipped and able to walk us through that moment, three people who had not experienced the loss and shock and suffering. How am I the one chosen for this? I feel so unqualified.

I can't find the words. I don't *have* the words to pray. I can only ask God why. I can only look at my husband and mother-in-law and sit in the tension of confusion and angst with them. I fall on my knees next to my mother-in-law, and I pray. I don't want to, but I do. I hand them my heart and hands as a meager offering of help and hope. I sit with her and beg the God who sits on the throne and who also lives in me to offer up balm for my wounded people. And so I pray, "The Lord is our Shepherd, . . .Yes, He is."

And He was. He was a shepherd before the phone call, as I walked my baby girl through the anxiety of whether death might happen to her grandpa. And He was a Shepherd after the phone call, as we all faced the reality that death *did*, in fact, happen. In both places Jesus walked us through the valley of the anxiety and the valley of the grief because He's a good Shepherd, willing to walk anywhere with and for His sheep.

What followed that day, that night, those weeks, were a tangible expression of such a Shepherd, of God's grace and mercy. We were carried by our church family like we were of the same blood. This is the power of the cross—it reconciles a people once lost and divided with no business being friends, much less family. We were sent care packages for the kids and helped in ways we could never explain or pay back. My father-in-law's years of serving the community spoke volumes as the outpouring of love was showered back on our family. He was a friend to everyone and hope to many. We were met with meals and words and prayers that carried us, held us, and healed us. This is Jesus's hands and feet running to help and heal; this is the bride being the palpable expression of God's grace and goodness. This is our Shepherd guiding His flock to come in close and warm the ones who face a terrible, cold, dark night of the soul.

I suppose I shouldn't be surprised. After all, it's not just Psalm 23 that reveals our God as a Shepherd. He shows up in so many places as a Shepherd in the Old Testament, and He promises that where human leaders fail and abandon the task, He'll show up *Himself* to guide His people (Ezek. 34:1–16). And you know what? He did just that by coming in the flesh to us. Jesus came down to earth and gathered His flock to Himself, blatantly calling Himself "the good shepherd." Hear His words to you:

> "I am the good shepherd. The good shepherd lays down his life for the sheep. The hired hand, since he is not the shepherd and doesn't own the sheep, leaves them and runs away when he sees a wolf coming. The wolf then snatches and scatters them. This happens because he is a hired hand and doesn't care about the sheep.

"I am the good shepherd. I know my own,
and my own know me, just as the Father
knows me, and I know the Father. I lay down
my life for the sheep." (John 10:11–15)

In just five verses, Jesus reminds you twice that *He's* the
good Shepherd you're looking for in times of trouble. Grief
might feel like a wolf to you in this season—a wave of it
around every corner to overwhelm you, sink its teeth into you,
and snatch you down under its powerful current. But where
many others might abandon you in that place of utter confusion and loss, Jesus won't. Why? Because you belong to Him.
He purchased you with His own blood, and now you are His.
He knows His own. And if you have erected a living Stone in
your story where you came to trust Him, *you are one of His
own.* When the wolf closes in, He says Himself that He won't
run for it. He'll stay, and He'll guide you through the danger.

Friend, Jesus is your help right now, your good Shepherd
through the grief and the loss, your Comforter. Kneeling with
you, holding your hands, carrying the suffering, and offering
supernatural peace and hope that could only come from Him.
This is Jesus, the God who meets us in our daily lives no matter what and no matter who. He's walking with you, giving
you a whole life full of all sorts of Ebenezer stones—even the
grieving stones—that reveal He keeps showing up. Not just
the moment of meeting Him *but in every hill and especially
every valley after that.*

I don't know what your grief and sorrow look like right
now, but He will walk with you through it. After all, the
Father doesn't just introduce us to the good Shepherd and then

tell us to go home. A shepherd is someone who guides you after you meet him, no matter where you go and no matter what the wolf looks like. He can meet you. He can stay. He can lead you through the grief. Even here. Because Jesus doesn't just guide you in a generic sense; He knows how to walk you through each specific valley, how to move through unbelief, suffering, and grief. He knows which way to lead you after a shattered dream, a ruined relationship, the loss of a loved one, or what seems to be an unanswered prayer. He knows how long the road needs to be, and He can light your darkness along the way. And even if you stumble and fall or hurt yourself, He will carry you through parts of the journey when you feel the weakest and unraveled. *He is your good Shepherd who meets you at your grieving stone.* Yes, He is.

The Sustainer Who Feeds

When I think back to that time of grief in my family, I remember lots of things. But you know what else I experience beyond just remembering the facts? I can *taste* some of the meals made for us like it was yesterday. Grief is that way. It comes with lots and lots of meals.

Some days we don't want to eat those meals. The loss leaves us hungry for only the lost person's presence, and food just doesn't come close to filling the ache. We just stare at a wall until days have gone by, and the fact that we haven't eaten in far too long seems to have escaped our notice. Those are the days we have to be force-fed by the good friends in our lives, for they know we need the sustenance if we're going to make it through the week. Other days we wake up ravenous, and we binge everything in the refrigerator. We know we can't fill the void of loss, but we desperately try to anyway.

See, bereavement knows nothing of balance or proper pacing. It just floods us and then lets up till we're numb, floods and lets up, floods and lets up. That's why we need an outside figure in our lives who knows how to sustain us in the madness of it all. We need that person who recommends broth when we're not hungry at all or broccoli when we've downed nothing but ice cream for a few days straight.

Many others may try to be this for us, but really, this person is Jesus. He's not just a shepherd who guides us through the season of loss but a *sustainer,* too. He sustains us during the moments we feel empty and void and nothing but loss. When we are weak and feeble, He nourishes us and helps us along. When we receive His words to us, we are galvanized inside, if even little by little. To precisely the point we need Him to in order to make it through this valley, He fortifies us. Hebrews 1:3 says He sustains *the whole universe,* including you and me, dear friend. Imagine that! He didn't just create the universe and walk away, wishing it the best of luck as it unwinds. He keeps it running every single second. He has the power to uphold it and keep it ticking. If He can do this for the universe, He can do it for you and me in our valleys, no matter how low the path takes us. He's a sustainer. Not only does He say, "I am the good shepherd," able to guide you on the journey through grief. He also says, "I am the bread of life," able to feed you along the way to keep your strength up.

Friend, grief may be draining you dry. It has done that to me too. So many times. But there is a sustainer who can meet you in that place and replenish you. When it's all too much and you feel you're going to slip into a deep, dark abyss, *He can uphold you.* Through this terrible patch of the journey, He can not only lead you; He can also feed you.

The Interceder and Advocate Who Pleads

There are many ways Jesus sustains us through grief (or any other season in life). Through His Word, His presence, His people, and so on. But you know one really crazy-cool way He is upholding us in the seasons of loss and darkness? As our Intercessor and Advocate. Did you know Jesus intercedes for you? Did you know He advocates for you? Don't take my word for it. Look at how the Bible itself describes this:

> Now many have become Levitical priests, since they are prevented by death from remaining in office. But because [Jesus] remains forever, he holds his priesthood permanently. Therefore, he is able to save completely those who come to God through him, **since he always lives to intercede for them.** (Heb. 7:23–25, emphasis added)

> My little children, I am writing you these things so that you may not sin. But if anyone does sin, **we have an advocate with the Father—Jesus Christ the righteous one.** He himself is the atoning sacrifice for our sins. (1 John 2:1–2, emphasis added)

Tell me this doesn't do something to your soul inside. I mean, here is our Jesus, raising up a banner of love for our souls. The one who intercedes for us always. The one who advocates for us before the Father's throne, even now.

What does all this mean? It means that Jesus didn't just stand in your place on the cross for your conversion. He now stands in your place every moment after that. An interceder offers up a request on behalf of another person, right? In their place. An advocate, similarly, makes a case on behalf of someone else. In their place.

Jesus didn't just die in your place and then hightail it out of the picture, leaving you to fend for yourself. No. In sunshine or storm Jesus stands in your place, lifting up His prayers and His advocacy on your behalf before the Father. That's what priests did in the Old Testament. They were the mediators who stood in the gap between the people and God. But priest after priest, well, died, and someone new had to take the role. But Jesus doesn't die. He's resurrected. He will live forever. And so He needs no replacement. *Forever forever forever* He will stand in your place and plead your cause. That's your Jesus, friend. *That's* your hope in the grief and the loss and the weight of it all. He won't just lead and feed; He will plead. For you. In your place. Right now. Always.

Relatable, Remember?

In the last chapter we learned that Jesus is the God who gets you. That's true in a general sense. I mean, it's a big deal that he wasn't just God but also human. The cross wouldn't mean anything unless both those things were true.

But the valley of grief—whew. I mean, that's not a "general" thing. Grief is a specific place of pain, and it's a place where this truth of "God becoming human" makes its way from "cool theology fact" to "huge difference in my life." Because, see, we can talk all day about Jesus being the Shepherd of the sheep and Feeder of the sheep and Interceder for the sheep and Advocate for the sheep. But it's another thing entirely to say, "Oh yeah, and He also knows what it's like to be the sheep in the equation too."

Doesn't that make you trust Him to be a good Shepherd? No one can guide a sheep like someone who knows what it's like to be one—you know, down there near the ground, amid the dirt and the rocks and the wolves. No one can feed a sheep quite like the one who has personally experienced the difference between the taste of a fresh, green pasture and dry, brown, dead grass. No one is a better interceder or advocate for the life of a weary little sheep than—you get the picture—the One who actually understands the daily exhaustion and dangers of such a creature.

Here's the news that makes all that other stuff about Jesus hit home: *He really did become a sheep.* As Isaiah says, He was the sheep who was led to the slaughter (Isa. 53:7). If anyone knows what it's like to be you, friend, it's Jesus. What makes Him the best Shepherd/Sustainer/Interceder/Advocate for you through your sorrow is the wild truth that He was a "man of sorrows" Himself (Isa. 53:3 NLT). He knows what your pain feels like. He knows that experience of sorrow washing over His soul in waves. He can be trusted with your sorrows and grief and loss because He's felt the depths of darkness that lives in that place. When He leads, feeds, and pleads as your Shepherd, Sustainer, and Advocate, He does so gently *as someone who's been there*. Think about it: Isn't that the kind of person you want leading you through the valley? Because Hebrews 4:15 says He has! He actually went before you and faced it head-on far before He ever asked you to! *Our God knows grief,* which is why we can trust Him in ours.

All that We Need

Want to see Jesus do these things in an example? There is a story in John 11 that puts these characteristics of Christ on full display.

Jesus receives a message that His friend Lazarus is severely ill. Lazarus's two sisters, Mary and Martha, seek the help of their friend Jesus. Surely, He can save their brother (John 11:3). When Jesus hears of this, He immediately encourages them with the truth that Lazarus's illness is not the end, and He begins to make His way to the town of Bethany. Upon His arrival, He is told that Lazarus has already passed away.

Tell me the following moments in the story speak don't deeply to your soul's human reality and honest condition:

> As soon as Mary came to where Jesus was and saw him, she fell at his feet and told him, "Lord, if you had been here, my brother wouldn't have died!"
>
> When Jesus saw her crying, and the Jews who had come with her crying, he was deeply moved in his spirit and troubled. "Where have you put him?" he asked.
>
> "Lord," they told him, "come and see."
>
> Jesus wept. (John 11:32–35)

"If you had been here!"

Oh Mary, I feel for you. I've said those words before. *Had He been there, had He interceded, had He done something about it.* Yet He has. And He did.

Jesus was right there. Not only was Jesus weeping with them; He also leaned in with holy compassion, making room for the entirety of their being, their wholeness, their brokenness, their doubt, their conflicted feelings—all of it. I picture Him sitting down with them, crying with them, feeling the weight of it, and saying, "I know it's a lot, but you're safe here." This is what He does with us in our grief. He feels it with us. And by the power of His presence, He brings back to life a withered soul, breathing hope and light into hopelessness and darkness. Let's let Him do this for our hearts and minds, friend. He knows grief but also knows hope. How can I say that? Because as you know, the story doesn't end with weeping. Jesus eventually prays to the Father and then calls Lazarus out of the grave (John 11:41–43). That's right. A dead man brought back to life.

That right there is why it's possible for you and me to grieve deeply but also grieve with hope and expectation. Because Jesus can breathe life into both the weeping Marys of the world and the dead Lazaruses. Sometimes it is by the simple comfort of His presence in the valley; other times it is by the miraculous power of His Word to deliver us from the thing causing us harm. Whether it takes the form of comfort or deliverance, one thing I know: Jesus will breathe life into your valley if you'll let Him.

Do you see how Jesus is all that we need in John 11? He is clearly the Shepherd of the situation. He decided the pacing of how this story would go and led each party to the place where they'd see His plan unfold. He is clearly the Sustainer, too—the one who met people in their pain and comforted them so that they might be fortified in a moment of total weakness. He was the Interceder and Advocate, as He prayed to the Father on their behalf and then brought a man back from the dead.

I can't know how Jesus will lead you through your valley. I can't know what instruction will be on His lips when you meet Him at your grieving stone. Whether He gives you comfort or deliverance, I know one thing: He will breathe life. *He will be all that you need.*

So, friend, don't avoid Him at your grieving stone. Let God meet you at it. Remember, in the valley the problem is not His inability to help or meet us, but often it is our reluctant will not to let Him in. He will be your good Shepherd. Your Sustainer. Your Intercessor and Advocate. He will prove Himself all that you need. *Go to the stone and trust Him to show up for you there.* He will.

A Forever Kind of God

For so long I'd thought that Jesus's work was finished for me when I said yes to following Him. Little did I know that He was just getting started. Our yes to Jesus isn't a one-time transaction but a lifelong relationship, moment to moment, Ebenezer to Ebenezer. As I've said before, the work of the cross wasn't only displayed for us to marvel at and then forget. It was a gift that forged the beginning of a lifelong journey with a God who is committed to walking with us every day of our lives. Your God is in this for the long haul, friend. He's a forever kind of God. And if you take the hand of Christ as your Shepherd, you cannot go the wrong way—even in the darkness and disorientation of grief.

You are an ordinary human as much as you are a special child of God. And God not only welcomes the feelings of anger, confusion, and sadness but sits with you in it. He doesn't leave you there though. Rather, He moves you forward—onward.

God will take even the most hurtful of circumstances and bring new life out of them. He'll even use them to help you become more like Him. I've seen it in my own life, and I see it in John 11, and I have the faith to see it in your story, too. What was once Lazarus's place of death and defeat turned into a place of compassion and hope and comfort and resurrection life. It was an Ebenezer to all who witnessed the events. It was their grieving stone, where they trusted Jesus enough to experience Him in a new way. It was a place they could look back on, knowing it carried the testament of a God who met His friends and His people there. It was a place of loss that ended up becoming a clear display of their leader, feeder, and pleader who was

Faithful

Loving

Gentle

Compassionate

Everything they needed.

That gravesite was a mile marker in their journey where they could remember the truth that we must remember at our

Grieving Stones, too—that our God is the God who cares, the God who sees, and the God who hears. He isn't merely standing by watching us endure hardships; He's actively involved in our healing. The Creator of the heavens and earth, the God of ages, the One who has carried and cared for our hearts since the beginning of time (Isa. 46:4). He's the comfort and the balm; He is the redemption and restoration. He's present in pain, actively mending the wounds we attempt to mend from human grit—with the precious blood of Jesus. He's not a bystander but our Protector and Healer. We must remember that Jesus weeps with us while holding and mending us back to wholeness. *He's good, and He's here.* His word tells us so. And you and I tell the stories, the echoes of God's mercy and grace in and through our lives. At the Grieving Stone, yes, and every other stone along the path of our journeys with Him. Hear this today, friend: *He loves you in your pain. He heals you in your anguish. He restores you from the brokenness.*

Looking Up

Mary and Martha and Lazarus met Jesus at their Grieving Stone. They let Him in, even with the hardest of questions they could throw at Him and the agony of it all. They watched Him show up for them. They saw God in the flesh, weeping with them and bringing new life into a lifeless situation. They let Him be their Shepherd, Sustainer, Intercessor, and Advocate.

Will you?

What's your Grieving Stone? I mean, we all have one (or for many of us, more than one). A place of pure loss and total confusion. I wonder, if you looked at the long path of your journey with God, and you could drop a pin for this stone in your story, where would it land? What situation would it be? What faces would be part of the story?

One of my grieving stones, as I've shared, is the loss of my father-in-law. It was terrible. But it is also a place I can now look back on and say God really did meet me in that stretch of the journey. You probably know exactly where that stone would land for you, but you might be fighting the call to drag such a painful memory out of the vault. I get that. But think about it. Taking the time to name your grieving stone gives you the chance to look up to the faithfulness of God and trace the ways He proved to be all that you needed, though you may not have been able to see it at the time. What if, now, you finally had eyes to see the ways He showed up and cared for you or built your endurance?

Friend, it is possible for that place of earthly defeat to simultaneously be a place you were met with heavenly hope. Because where there is defeat, there is always hope, and His name is Jesus. And He works through the whirlwind of life—even in the hurt. He is not scared off by that stuff. Where we are engulfed with pain, He not only meets us in it, but He also builds up in us resolve and spiritual endurance and gives us in return for our pain a faith unshaken.

So don't be afraid to mark this moment in your story, this stone of grief where Jesus showed up. The road may not look like you wanted it to, I know. The loss might be very real. The dream might be shattered, the loved one lost, a part of your heart or mind bruised and battered by the storms of life. But your Jesus gets it. He has walked that road before you did, and He understands its twists and turns and the unexpected patches of thorns that cut deep. The fact that He not only understands the valley on a personal level but draws near to you in it, shepherds you through it, sustains you as you walk it, intercedes for you when you're weak, and advocates for you when you need help—that right there proves He's good to you. He wouldn't have done all that if He weren't good! Even if the *road* did not end up being all you wanted or needed, *Jesus* did.

Maybe He met you through people who acted similarly to the people in my story, showing up in seasons of loss and sustaining you with meals or words of encouragement. Perhaps He did it through Scripture, which proved to be a balm for your soul or the clear direction you needed from the Shepherd. Maybe He did it through His felt presence as He did with Mary—a time when you know in your soul He was drawing Himself close to you in the worst of moments. Maybe He did it through a gift card dropped off or a random check in the mail at just the right time or words of wisdom from a seasoned believer who saved you from going even further down a road of danger or a song sung at a funeral that was clearly from heaven, straight to you. I can't possibly know how He was there—that's for you to chart in your own story—but I know, friend, *He was there*.

Look for evidence of His presence. Why? Because He wants nothing more than for you to see His hand and heart in your life. He wants you to see His sovereignty practically work itself out for your good and His glory from something you could not even imagine would be life giving, God, or good. If you need to borrow some of my hope and faith to help you take a chance and look for His hand at work in your life, you can. You can borrow the hope and faith of those who have seen Him move while you try to mark His hand in your own life. Here it is—I'm handing it to you. This is one of the gifts of the family of God—we can borrow hope and faith when we feel like we have none.

So, using your own faith or borrowed faith, decide right now to stop and chart it. Somewhere in your story there is a Grieving Stone you can raise as an Ebenezer. Where is it? Where can you lift your eyes and say, "Jesus met me in this loss and pain and sustained my soul?" Where can you look back and realize, "I couldn't see it at the time, but He really was shepherding me through the pain." Drop that pin in the map of your testimony, dear friend, for this is yet another Ebenezer moment that gives shape to your story—*the Lord brought you this far.* He was leading you, feeding you, and pleading for you in this valley *right here.* I mean it. Give it a name, and mark it in your story. I can wait. I'll be right here when you return.

Now, here's the great part of what you just did. You not only got to process an important moment of your story, but now you also have a memorial to fall back on when the next wave of grief comes over you. No matter how deep the loss goes, no matter what that next season of pain might look like, you can look back on this Ebenezer moment where Christ met you, guided you, and sustained you. One day you'll need the reminder that Jesus can meet you in the hard places, and because of what you did today, you'll have that reminder marked in your journey, clear as day. You'll have all the proof you need that your story holds evidence of His goodness and grace, and you'll have the confidence to say: "He has, indeed, shown up before, and He'll do it again." And He will.

■ ■ ■

When God led me to read Psalm 23 for Leilla that night, it was His shepherding hand.

When I prayed Psalm 23 in the hospital room, it was His intercessory hand.

When our church body leaned in and covered us like the ocean blue, it was His sustaining hand.

And all of it was His heart.

Tracing those moments, painful as it is for me, reveals the handprints of God in the dark places the world says He could never possibly be at work. But what the world can't understand is just how much the Shepherd loves the sheep and just how familiar He is with the valley. You and I are the loved ones, and as a good shepherd does, our Jesus will not leave us or let even one of us go astray or remain alone. Our friend Jesus isn't afraid of the valley. He carries the grief and hurt of our souls right smack-dab in the middle of it. Tracing His hand reveals this about His heart. So trace it, and enjoy the blessed assurance of the God who lays us down beside still waters and carries the heavier load so that we might make it to the next stone, and the next, and the next.

EYES UP

Lift your eyes and look back on your own journey, taking the time to chart this crucial moment (or season) in your life.

1. When it comes to grief, what is your default response to it? How do you cope? Why?

2. What is your grieving stone? How did God meet you in your pain? In what ways did He undo some things in you, and though it was painful, He proved faithful?

3. In this chapter we learned that Jesus is the good Shepherd, Sustainer, Interceder, and Advocate. Which of these spoke most to your heart? Why?

4. Jesus personally understands grief. Why is this important for you to know as you face your own seasons of grief?

5 The Stone on the Mountaintop

How to Fight the Bad that Hides in the Good

If there are valleys, then there must also be mountaintops.

I've just finished sweeping up the remanent of taco Tuesday's cheese and lettuce from the floor when I suddenly burst into tears. I quickly make my way to the one room in the house where I can find solitude—my closet—and instantly fall on my knees.

It feels like I've been in this valley for a decade. "God, will there ever be a moment of rest or good?" My prayers are short. "God, please, help me." I don't have the energy to lift up an explanation to God on why my heart is weary. Honestly, it's too painful to even try to put words to it. It's the type of pain that runs deep in the soul, the kind that only you and God understand, the one communicated best through tears and prayer. And frankly, speaking of God, I'm feeling irritated and bitter toward Him—so naturally, my first response isn't to pour my heart out the way I would in a season of sweet intimacy with Him. Plus, I also tell myself under my breath, "He already knows how I feel, doesn't He?" Yet I am in the closet, searching for answers and revival from a God I am also actively trying to avoid.

The help I'm asking for is nuanced—there are layers to it. It isn't just one problem but several. I wait and pray again and wonder if my words are making their way to the only One who can bring relief. Prayers are typically words of thanksgiving, adoration, holy confessions, and contemplations, the moments in which we decide to remind our heart and mind that we are not the ones who are in control—but God. Today though, right now, my prayers are simply supplications mixed in with despair and distrust.

See, for several weeks I'd found myself advocating for one of my kiddos to get the support they needed at school but to no avail. On top of that I'd been advocating for myself at work—tenaciously standing my ground for my dignity and worth after learning that one of my coworkers had disparaged my character in ways that had triggered every ounce of child-hood trauma. And on top of all that, I was gripping for the strength to keep going as I helped my mother, who was in a traumatic season, too, find healing and restoration of her own. And yet there was more I was bearing. A grieving husband and children—the death of my father-in-law still stings for us all.

Have you ever had a season like that? So many trials are working in tandem? For some reason the challenges of life usually show up like this—all at once. I needed a sign from God, a burning bush to remind me that God is who He says He is, holy and good—unchanging, gentle, and compassion-ate. But instead of waiting for it, all I want to do is run away because the mountain standing between me and reprieve seems unmovable—I've tried everything to move it.

A million little trials. *But in the same season, when I look back, I see there were also a million little miracles.*

A text message came the morning after I'd found myself pleading with God. We'd been gifted some time away at a beach just a few hours away. It came through the Monday morning walk of some friends we have.

"Hey, Alex, this might seem wild, but this morning my husband and I were on a walk and could not shake the feeling that God wants your family here to rest. We want to gift you our home for a few days."

I hadn't spoken to this friend in some time. How did she know? A few weeks later we make our way down and are gifted a million little miracles while we're there—moments of healing and of joy. This doesn't always happen in seasons of stress, but it did this time.

We made it down to their place right before sunset—the sky looks like what I imagine heaven to be. A canvas painted by the uncreated Creator. I stand looking out to the ocean and think to myself, *The God over all is the God that covers all.* And I breathe deeply, inhaling His peace and exhaling my angst. My oldest daughter is sitting on the sand right next to me as her siblings build sandcastles with their dad. Leilla then looks up at me and says, "Mom, remember when you told me that God's love is like the ocean—you can see its beginning but not its end? I think I know what you mean now. It goes on forever."

God's love—for a moment, I almost miss the gift of this Ebenezer—our friends' generous hearts and also my daughter's words.

I don't know what "mountaintop" moments look like for you. But that day at that house on that beach with those words from my daughter, well, that was one of the most impactful mountaintop moments. Where in the middle of my mess God brought about deep soul rest. We were healing and mending; this was answered prayer. God heard me in that closet. I know it. The evidence was right in front of me. A home at no cost for several days and a peace that surpassed my understanding. A glimpse of God's grace in the middle, showing us His hand to remind us of His heart. Up high enough to see things from His point of view, giving us a different vantage point to things we are often too close to see.

These mountaintop moments, for me, teach me that we must have farsighted faith in a nearsighted world. This small and slightly inconspicuous moment can become a holy one, where God meets us and brings about reprieve in a way that our souls desperately need.

I know my little story about that house and that day on the beach is not your typical mountaintop moment, but you know what I've learned? Most of them won't be. Most will be small, almost unassuming moments that may feel like luck or even coincidence. Others will feel like hard work and grit. Either way, they are all God.

"I've brought you this far."

Mountaintop God

The mountain is a familiar place when we look through the pages of Scripture. God does some amazing things from mountains: God reveals Himself to Abraham on a mountain (Gen. 22), He lets Moses in on His upcoming plans for redemption on a mountain (Exod. 3), and He gives His people His life-giving law through Moses on a mountain (Exod. 19–20). When we look to the New Testament, we see that Jesus does some great things from mountains, too. He resists Satan on a mountain (Matt. 4:8), meets with His Father often on mountains, teaches from the mountainside, and was likely crucified on a mountain. And after He was resurrected, He even proclaims the Great Commissions from a mountain! (Matt. 28:16). No matter where we find a mountain in Scripture, *God is there. Doing unbelievable things.* And the same is true for the "mountains" in our lives. God is still there, still present, still doing amazing things. He has met us not only in the valleys, as we explored in the last chapter, but on our mountaintop experiences too. His hand is at work down low *and* up high.

The problem is, we forget this. So we must look up.

In Deuteronomy 8:1–18, we find Moses giving the Israelites wise words concerning the posture of their hearts. Considering they'd just been delivered from the wilderness and their natural bent toward pride and idolatry, Moses had to give them some guardrails of truth to live from and remember. In the first few verses, he reminds them of how far they've come by inviting them to remember. He knew the age-old truth that sometimes we have to look back in order to fully move forward. For the Israelites that meant pausing to remember all God had done for them up until now: the miraculous supplies of food, the protection, the deliverance from Egypt, the strength for their journey. This moment of remembrance served as a good reminder for all the ways, through both God's providence and grace, He had led His people through that season. And the same is helpful for us to do sometimes as well. We have to be reminded of the valleys we were once brought from to help us experience the fullness of what God has brought us to now.

Hear how Moses helps them recall all that God had done for them in the valley:

> Remember that the LORD your God led you on the entire journey these forty years in the wilderness, so that he might humble you and test you to know what was in your heart, whether or not you would keep his commands. He humbled you by letting you go hungry; then he gave you manna to eat, which you and your ancestors had not known, so that you might learn that man does not live on bread alone but on every word that comes from the mouth of the LORD. Your clothing did not wear out, and your feet did not swell these forty years. (Deut. 8:2–4)

God's people had made it so very far. Where they were once enslaved under the oppression of Egypt, they were now free. They were now about to enter an entirely new, fruitful season. They had made it through a forty-year valley, and

they'd soon be experiencing the mountaintop. Hear how good
God's plans were for the season just ahead of them:

> So keep the commands of the LORD your God
> by walking in his ways and fearing him. For
> the LORD your God is bringing you into a
> good land, a land with streams, springs, and
> deep water sources, flowing in both valleys
> and hills; a land of wheat, barley, vines, figs,
> and pomegranates; a land of olive oil and
> honey; a land where you will eat food without
> shortage, where you will lack nothing; a land
> whose rocks are iron and from whose hills
> you will mine copper. When you eat and are
> full, you will bless the LORD your God for the
> good land he has given you. (Deut. 8:6–10)

Here's the deal: the Israelites knew they needed God in
the seasons of the valley. We all do, right? We have no other
choice but to reach out to Him for help. But would they need
God just as much in their mountaintop season? Would they
remember Him there? Or could they sit back and coast for a
while? They had made it through the dangers of the valley, but
what about the mountaintop—were there any dangers there
that they'd need God to help them through?

Let's read verses 11–18 to hear God's answer:

> **"Be careful** that you don't **forget the LORD
> your God** by failing to keep his commands,
> ordinances, and statutes that I am giving you
> today. When you eat and are full, and build

beautiful houses to live in, and your herds and flocks grow large, and your silver and gold multiply, and everything else you have increases, **be careful** that your heart doesn't become proud and you **forget the LORD your God** who brought you out of . . . the place of slavery. He led you through the great and terrible wilderness. . . . He brought water out of the flint rock for you. He fed you in the wilderness with manna. . . . You may say to yourself, 'My power and my own ability have gained this wealth for me,' **but remember that the LORD your God** gives you the power to gain wealth, in order to confirm his covenant he swore to your ancestors, as it is today. If you ever **forget the LORD your God** and follow other gods to serve them and bow in worship to them, I testify against you today that you will certainly perish." (Deut. 8:11–19, emphasis added)

The answer is plain as day: *Yes,* there are dangers on top of the mountain, just as there were dangers in the valley. They may look different, but there are toils and snares in every season. "Be careful!" Moses wouldn't say this twice if he didn't think a real danger was in store for the people as they enter their season of respite and fruitfulness.

So, what's the type of danger the Israelites need God to show up for this time? Is it bread and water and deliverance like last time? Nope. Look closely at how many times the passage says "forget the LORD your God." Three times! *Forgetfulness.* That's the big danger in a season of plenty. Why? Because forgetfulness makes you proud (v. 14).

See, God had not saved or chosen the Israelites by their own merit, obedience, or work—rather, by His own grace (Deut. 7:7). They were a part of a bigger story, and His love covered them in it. *God* is the One who led His people through the dark days, but God would be the one to lead them through their mountaintop experiences, too. If they'd only remember that He was the One helping them through both.

The temptation of pride is too great in moments of forgetfulness—which is why a posture of thanksgiving and gratitude must be our resolve. Like the Israelites, many of us remember that God is the One who has led us through the valleys, but yet we are so tempted to forget Him when He lifts us up to the mountaintop. God warns the Israelites—and us—especially in verse 17, not to assume our hands are what got us to this place of prosperity. *Recall your Ebenezers, beloved. I'm the One who brought you this far.*

Don't Forget

Just like the Israelites and just like me, God has done immeasurably more in your life than you could ever imagine and provided in ways you will never understand. And one day you'll reach a part of your story where you'll see Him move in mighty ways, and you'll be tempted to think that it was the work of your hands that got you there. But don't forget who brought the bounty. Don't think it was the work of your hands that brought you this far. Don't forget *why* God has brought you this far. The why for you is the same as the why for the Israelites: establishing His covenant and His plan for reconciling a people to Himself—to further His eternal purpose of a family made up of believers from every nation, tribe, and tongue. In some way or another, any season of prosperity in your life or my life or the lives of those Israelites is worked by the hand of God to achieve this greater goal.

And while we're talking about prosperity, what is the most prosperous place, really? I think it's being right in the middle of God's favor. So let's remember it is not the work of our hands that keeps us in this place of favor but the work of Christ on the cross that carries us there and keeps us there. Our performance and grit did not save us in our conversion, nor can it outdo God's will and grace in every season after that. We can give it all we've got on this side of heaven, and it will still be God who brings the increase, who brings the rain, and the God who makes the way.

Every good thing in our life is from God. Every good thing around us is from God. Every good thing that's ever happened, every good thing that's ever been or will be is the hand of God and grace in our lives. Remember, He's the God who knows, *yada*. The High Priest who experiences our grief and pain, the One who has felt it all for all. He knows your pain and aches, the tears. He's held them, each one, in the valley. And He's also the God who knows the joy of the good times. He knows how splendor and delight and rest feel. Our Jesus is reigning right now, experiencing those things at the right hand of the Father. Yet there's more. He's also the God who knows the in-between seasons. The ones that feel boring or monotonous or ordinary. Jesus faced those seasons, too, toiling away at project after project in His carpentry work during His earthly lifetime, tending to the younger siblings and earning another day's wages. He knows *all* these seasons, and in His wisdom, He bestows them on us depending on what we need to learn and when. In every single one of them, like I said, He's the one who knows the road and makes the way through it. He's the one who can open our eyes to see our mountaintop moments, even if we couldn't see them before, as His hand at work in our lives.

What if we counted even the smallest of coincidences, luck, or flukes as God's hand at work in our lives? What if we learned to take notice? My hope here is to invite you to see the ways in which God has not only walked you to the mountaintop but also the touch of grace that marked each moment. The mountaintop isn't always the medical break-through you're looking for, the Hallmark-movie-level proposal for marriage from your dream man, the mended relationship, the new job, or the unexcepted financial blessing (although all of those things are meaningful and useful and can well be a moment of God's grace!). More often than not, mountaintop moments are the ones you look back to in hindsight, realizing just how valuable they were in your story, though you couldn't see it at the time. They serve as sacred reminders. Moments in the ministry of the mundane that gave you revelation of His character, grace, and kindness. It is God who gets us to these moments, who brings us this far. And when we have eyes to see them for what they are, we realize that every step of the way has always been a grace where we learn to see Him, and for a minute, we stand there and catch our breath while God hands us a moment's rest from the hike that it took our soul to get there.

I've come to believe that our mountaintop moments include the obvious blessings and answers to prayer and flashy breakthroughs, *but they also include* the moments of grace that carry us from one moment to the next. Grace keeps us when nothing else can, and the cross carries us when nothing else will—valley or peak. And if grace carried you in a certain pivotal moment in your journey, well, that should count as a high point, right? That sounds like a place in the story where we remember to give God the credit.

But a lot of times we don't. When we get to the mountaintop, we struggle just like the Israelites did. When a season of prosperity—or even just a much-needed season of "boring and normal"—lies before us, we are often too tired or too blind to see it was God's hand guiding us the whole time. Instead, we tend to believe it was *our* hand and our hard work that got us there. As I mentioned before, it can be easy to say, "When I walk through the valley, You're with me"—after all, sometimes no one else but God will walk with you in such a deep, dark place. But we forget to say the equivalent statement when we're out of the woods: "When I walk on the mountaintop, You're with me there, too." I mean, we all want a shepherd for the valley. Who doesn't? But we want to go it alone once we're out! *Whew—thanks for getting me through that rough patch, God, but I've got it from here!*

Have you ever felt that way? Have you ever forgotten it is God's job to guide you in the low moments *and* the high ones? That His power can protect you from the dangers in both places? That when you look back over your life, you should see Ebenezer stones erected down in the dark places and also up in the heights?

The question, then, naturally arises: Why can't we remember God in the good times? Why is it so easy to forget Him? I think of two reasons: (1) because we don't really believe there are any threats to watch out for in the good times, and (2) because we don't know (or believe) God's heart for us in the good times.

The Hidden Bad in the Good Times

What do you think of when the word *success* is put in front of you? Extra money in the bank account? A promotion at work? An A+ on the test? A conflict-free marriage? Getting a husband? Lots of followers online? A booming ministry? Obedient kids? Being famous? A job that finally fits your gifts? A tidy house?

I don't know what success looks like for you, but rarely do we imagine it with threats or dangers in the picture. We just naturally assume successful seasons are void of struggle, sin, risks, or prowling enemies. Valleys, bad. Mountaintops, good. That's just how we think. But nothing could be further from the truth. Every season involves a mix of good and bad, including successful seasons. Every season includes things to enjoy and things to watch out for.

As we said before, the danger of the good times is forgetfulness that leads to pride. *So, what's the real danger in pride when you're in a season of prosperity?* you might wonder. *I mean, what's the worst that could happen?*

Well, the total ruin of everything you love, for starters.

Just think of our friend King Solomon in the Bible. He got all the mountaintop experiences a person could ask for in life. Wisdom, wealth, prosperity, attention, glory, status, marriage, kids, influence, health—you name it. And yet he finished terribly in life. He was not vigilant to follow God as his guide in the later seasons of his life while experiencing such prosperity. Because he was unwilling to steadily follow God through the good season, his heart was turned away from the Lord, toward idols, in the end. As Jesus would say, he gained the world but lost his soul. He got success in the world's eyes, but he lost God. And he eventually hurt *a lot* of people in doing so. God's warning in Deuteronomy 8:19 proved true. Solomon forgot to remember God, turned toward idols, and just as God said would happen, Solomon perished.

The peak of success can be even more dangerous than the valley, friend. The glitz and glimmer of the flashy seasons can be just as blinding as the darkness. At least in the valley we know to clutch on tight to God's hand for guidance. We stick close to His side. Even when we're angry or wounded, we know there's nowhere else to go. But in the abundant season, we slowly let go of His hand and begin to trust our own instincts. It was dark before, but now we think we can see. Except we can't. We get distracted by this glimmer over here and that flashy thing over there, just as Solomon did. And instead of eyes looking straight at God, our head is on a swivel, and we start wandering this way and that. Things may feel less intense than they did in the valley, but dangers are lurking in the good times that only God can see, and to be faithful there we must look up to Him all the more.

So let's take His warning to the Israelites. Let's remember Him. Not just in hell or high water but in paradise, too. And here's the real piece of encouragement in all of it: we should remember God in seasons of success not just because we are supposed to but because His heart for us in the high points of our journey *really is good*.

God's Heart for Us in the Good Times

We know that God goes through a lot of trouble to warn us about the dangers of taking credit for the "good times." And we know what happens to a person who doesn't heed His warning. So in all the sharp words God uses to warn us, what's His end game? To keep us from having fun? To not let us fully enjoy the good times? To make us fearful every step of the way?

No! God warns us to remember Him in the good times because *He wants us to finish strong*. He knows the end result of people who grow apathetic or calloused in the mountaintop seasons—they will perish. And He doesn't want that to be the end of your story or mine. He doesn't want us to perish in our apathy but to *vibrantly live*. He wants *life* for us, not death. Remembering God's hand at work on the mountaintop, friend, protects us against Solomon's fate and helps us continue to rely on God's kind guidance through the toils and snares of success.

Our God is the God of both feast and famine. This is the faithfulness of God's heart. He gives us provision and grace in every season because He finds it within His own nature to do so. Our being in God rescues us—not our doing. This is

God's heart for us, that in the highs and lows we can learn to
see His hand, trust His heart, and give Him the glory for it.

Don't get me wrong. Times of prosperity can be so refreshing. I think about that moment on the beach and the words
of my daughter, and heaven knows that felt like the splash of
refreshment I needed in such a hard stretch of the road. And
I have so many more mountaintop moments I could list—
breakthroughs in my marriage, work situations sorted out so I
could use my gifts, friendships mended, health restored after
sickness. But *remembering God's hand* in such times is crucial,
else we will probably let our good gifts become idols we worship instead of blessings we give God credit for.

We have a choice between two paths when the good times
roll in: respond like Solomon did or respond like James tells
us to, reminding ourselves that every good and perfect gift
comes from the Father's hand, not our own (James 1:17). If
we rob God of His glory, we will miss out on the Ebenezer left
for us in the middle of the miracle. If we take credit for one
blessing, we will take it for all, making ourselves the God and
hero of our story—which we are not. Pride will creep in, sure
as day. And so, friend, *the way to wage war against our pride is
to remember God's grace, and His name is Jesus.* May we give the
God who brought us this far the glory. He brings the bounty.
And His heart for us is good.

Choosing to remember the goodness of God only works
when you have something good to remember. What good
things can you remember? What mountaintops come to
mind? Maybe you're in a season of despair, where you just
can't remember. If you don't know what to look to, let me help
you see grace. Let me remind you of something true for us

all—something good God most definitely did in your life: the cross of Christ and His resurrection. Because friend, when we see all our debt paid, when we see an empty tomb that defeats death and darkness, when we see a Father fueled by love, then we can be anchored in the truth that God has always been for us, and God will always be with us.

Remember with me. Remember what's true of Him. Remember that God's heart for us in the good times is the same as it was in the dark times—see Him there, standing with us, proving Himself faithful. Remember the moments you couldn't keep going but God provided a way out of the valley and up the mountain, and give Him glory. I will, too. I am remembering those seasons right this very moment, right alongside you. And it's worth it. Because the more we do this, the more we remember, the more we get loud in our hearts and minds about the way we've seen God move. We get lost in His love, saturating ourselves with truth we'll need when a new valley or a new peak begins to make its way known. We may not be able to recreate mountaintop moments, but we can rehearse God's faithfulness. We can hide this in our hearts and replay it in our minds. We can remember God.

Sometimes the problem isn't that we can't remember the times God brought prosperity along. Sometimes the problem is the fact that in every waking moment we're in a hurry. We fail to remember not because the memory isn't there but because we don't take the time to slow down long enough to notice God's kindness. So slow down. Think for just a few seconds. Recall past moments that carry an aroma of good and make sure to ascribe them to God's grace. Don't miss out on what this does for your soul. Don't miss out on the blessing of remembrance. I know I missed out on seeing God's grace so much before that day at the beach—I'd lost sight of the truth that *God with us* gives every good gift. I had forgotten that He'd given me these moments of refreshment as arrows, pointing me back to Him.

No matter what kind of season you are in and no matter what struggle you carry in this stretch of the journey, here's the truth: one day we will see God reconcile all the things in the valley that don't make sense. And one day our eyes will be opened to the ways He protected us from all the mountaintop dangers we couldn't see. I know we're charting some of them in this book, but one day we'll see *all* the times God met us, helped us, and healed us. Even the ones we can't make out right now. Friend, one day we'll see it all, but until then let's remember that He's a safe place to land and He's got a strong hand to lead. Although we walk through the valleys, we're also led to the mountaintops. And it is because of God's heart that we ever even got there. It's a powerful and permanent truth. God is actually good and cannot be anything less.

Looking Up

Our mountaintops moments shouldn't escape our notice. The Ebenezer moments to be memorialized, places where God has helped us! And there are so many of those, friend. Let's trace the places He met us in the heights. Breathe in His peace and presence. Remember that He's not capable of anything but being perfect, loving, righteous, and good. Take a step back and ask Him to give you farsighted vision for just a second, to give it all a good look, because every good gift comes from God. God is good, and God is good to you. *Evidence of this is in your story.*

By now you've got the gist of this book—you know what I'm going to ask you to do. So here I am, asking. What mountaintop moment can be memorialized in your life as an Ebenezer? If your life were a long winding road, where on the path could you drop down a stone of remembrance where God proved Himself faithful in a time of success? Where is there evidence that He met you in the good times?

Chart it. Right now. Listen to God's warning and *remember Him.* Fill in your story with yet another stone. Remember the ways He got you to this time of prosperity or breakthrough. Put it down, right in front of your eyes, so you can return to it the next time you question whether He's able to lead you through not just the hard times but the good times, too. Raise your next Ebenezer! Lift your eyes to it. *God helped you this far.* He was good to you, *right here* on this place in the map of your life. I can count not just one of these moments in my life but many. More and more are coming to my mind . . . a million little miracles.

I wonder, *How many for you?*

EYES UP

Lift your eyes and look back on your own journey, taking the time to chart this crucial moment (or season) in your life.

1. What are general ways the world defines *success*?

2. What parts of that definition do you disagree with? What parts do you sometimes incorporate into your own version of success? Be specific.

3. Has anyone ever taken credit for something you did? How did that make you feel? How does this memory influence your reading of God's warning in Deuteronomy 8?

4. What misbeliefs do you need to release about God's heart for you in the good times (or the bad times)?

5. What Ebenezer stone has God built in your life on the mountaintop? How did He meet you in the heights? How might you better worship Him for being faithful, even there?

The Gravestone

6

Faith that Lives Where It Should Have Died

"This marriage was a mistake."

I couldn't breathe. Mario and I were eight years into our marriage, and our first child had just turned five. We were on a date, attempting to catch our breath from the unending demands of life. My soul was worn. I remember staring at him and asking, "How did we get here? How after so many years of counseling and grieving and working toward something better did you then decide that we were no longer a good fit?"

We were like oil and water. Two different people with two completely different backgrounds and, at the time, different beliefs and moral compasses. I'd broken Mario's heart, as he had broken mine. We lacked each other's trust. He believed the worst after I'd confessed some struggles I'd had with lust. In self-protection against the pain, he had used his words and lack of empathy as weapons. In my own ways, I weaponized my personality and words too. We'd hurt each other so deeply, and we weren't just hanging on by a thread; we were at a breaking point.

We could have given up, but we had chosen to stay—in our marriage, in our church, in our faith. Life was still hard, of course, but after enough time and persistence, I thought we were on the upswing. I thought I had done everything in my power to rebuild the trust that had been shattered. But maybe I was wrong. Maybe there were too many pieces to put back together.

I remember wondering to myself, *How do you get so far, to then look back and count it all a loss? Where was God in this?*

There's nothing like a crisis to take you down, and sitting there on that date, I was having one. A crisis in my faith and life.

A *crisis* by definition is "an unstable or crucial time or state of affairs in which a decisive change is impending; especially one with the distinct possibility of a highly undesirable outcome, or a situation that has reached a critical phase." At this point in our marriage, and in my faith overall, both these definitions were hitting the nail on the head. In marriage both our hearts had grown cold toward each other, edging God out and finding just about any reason to believe the worst, waiting for the undesirable outcome. We'd lost faith; we'd lost hope; we'd lost ourselves.

Often we turn a blind eye to the spaces in our life that God is asking us to notice, for the sake of not wanting to see what is so evidently hiding in plain sight. I knew that it would lead to a crisis if I asked Mario how he felt about our marriage, about me. I wondered if he was struggling to believe that I was no longer the eighteen-year-old he met way back when, if he still saw me as unfaithful and impure. More than that, if

God saw me that way. I was experiencing a crisis, but it wasn't like any I'd ever experienced before. It was a crisis of faith—of life itself. A crisis that left me wondering, *If God is good, then maybe He really isn't good to me.*

But a crisis of faith does not mean a faith forever lost. We sometimes misinterpret the challenges of life to mean God's unwillingness to care for us. At least I did in that moment. I anchored my faith in the very thing Scripture warns against—finding it in the hands of people over the One I'd found my hope in to begin with.

But I'm getting ahead of myself.

Like a lot of losses in life, the loss of faith in our marriage and in each other had happened gradually, chipping away at the trust we had entrusted to each other. After all, most changes don't happen overnight. Word by word, action by action (or lack thereof), we both began to pull away. Finding safety in isolation, protecting the last bit of life we both had inside our bones.

I couldn't see God, His hand, or His activity. Have you ever had a season like that? Where, no matter how good your physical vision might be, you are blind to God's presence, His hand, His help? I couldn't see anything in this darkness. It wasn't just a dimly lit valley—we've all been through those. This was that blinding kind of darkness that does nothing but make you terrified as you reach out for anything sturdy to help you find your way as you stumble forward, wondering if you're even headed the right direction. Wondering if you should even keep walking at all. Fear crippled me at the thought that maybe God *hadn't* brought me this far, that perhaps any good in my history was all coincidence, happenstance. I was afraid of being abandoned by the God who said He'd be the one who would carry me, carry *us*.

Unfortunately, I knew this feeling all too well—wondering if the rejection of someone in my life had to do with my lack or my past. Had I not done enough for God? Was this simply a game for Him? Had I not given my life over to King Jesus, who mends the brokenhearted and heals the sick? My wondering had turned to doubt, my doubt to disbelief. *Where are You, God? Why have You left me all alone?*

I could feel the pull at my heart—it was so strong. Like an undercurrent as mighty as a hurricane, and me, a sitting duck, helpless against its power. *You should turn back, Alexandra. You should hang up this whole "Christian" thing, and let it be some long-lost phase you went through in your past. You should walk away. After all, look where it got you. Right here in the dark.*

I don't know how else to explain that season in my spiritual journey other than to say it was the moment I should have put my whole faith in the tomb. *It was the moment my circumstances should have put a nail in the coffin of the whole "Jesus" season of my life.*

Maybe you know exactly what I'm talking about because you've been there before, too. Or maybe you're there right now. Maybe you know exactly what the cold and the blackness all around feels like because you're sitting in it right this minute.

Like I was, you're not in a valley. You're in a tomb. You're in that moment of the journey where faith goes to die, and you're wondering if God is there, if Jesus is truly who He says He is, if any of this is real.

Call it deconstruction or deconversion or a crisis of faith, but this, my friend, is the point in the Christian journey called the gravestone. Mine culminated on a date with my husband. Yours might take a million different shapes. But the place is the same for the both of us. A terrible quiet hangs in the air. The stench of lifelessness does, too, as your trust in God begins to breathe its last. It's pure darkness no matter which way you look. Are you only a step ahead of your last Ebenezer moment? Are you just one step shy of your next one? Or have you lost the path altogether? Will your faith make it, or is this the place your faith goes to die and you just start a new life without God, ditching the whole Christianity thing? There's no way to tell. Because when the gravestone is rolled over any light and the tomb holds you captive in total darkness, *you can't see.*

Jesus Has Been There

I often think about how Jesus Himself faced this sort of moment in Luke 22. Do you remember where He was when He was so anxious He sweat drops of blood? It was the garden of Gethsemane, before the betrayal of Judas and right before the cross. He was in crisis, in that wrestling moment with the Father, wondering, *Is this the way it really has to be? Isn't there some other way?* His prayer of distress lifted up to heaven:

> "Father, if you are willing, take this cup away
> from me." (v. 42)

Can't you feel His agony? I mean, who wants to face the pain of death and the darkness of the grave? No one. Not even God in the flesh. *Take this away, Father. I don't want to be here. I don't want to face a grave.*

And so, what does He do? Where does He lean with the weight and anxiety of it all? What is His reaction when the darkness is closing in and the depth of crisis is lower than any typical valley in His life thus far?

> Being in anguish, he prayed more fervently.
> (v. 44)

In the blackness that blinded Him from all around, Jesus leaned into His Father. When He couldn't force God's hand to take the circumstance away, He trusted God's heart. He proves as much if we pay attention to His words of resolve and faith at the end of His prayer:

> "Nevertheless, not my will, but yours, be done." (v. 42)

Can you see Him? There He was, standing in between two gardens, one that holds the grief of what is and one that holds out in front of Him what will be—a future, heavenly Eden, which promises to make all things right (Rev. 22:1–2). Days away from death but also life. This momentary yet life-shattering affliction had been passed through God's knowledge and God's hand, and this is where Jesus anchored His faith—in His Father's heart over the face of His gravestone moment.

And Jesus didn't just do this a couple of days before His death. He did it in His last breaths, too—in those moments He didn't just *feel* like He might deconstruct but when His body *actually* broke down and died. Do you remember? His words there on the cross are similar to the garden moment, starting with anguish as he wrestled with His Father: "My

God, my God, why have you abandoned me?" (Matt. 27:46).
If you've ever wondered where God was in your darkest crisis
moment, friend, be encouraged. Jesus did, too.

But He doesn't end there. After the wrestle comes the
white flag. After the struggle comes the yielding. The surrender. "And Jesus called out with a loud voice, 'Father, into your
hands I entrust my spirit.' Saying this, he breathed his last"
(Luke 23:46).

Jesus feels abandoned. In a moment of utter agony, He
digs deep and tells the truth of what this circumstance makes
Him feel. *Given up on. Left. Alone. Stupid. Abandoned.
Ashamed.* He doesn't try to clean up and make things sound
good. He doesn't put on a smile. He tells the Father, plain as
day—*in public,* no less—all of that terrible, dark, miserable
stuff going on inside of Him. In the crisis He's honest to the
point of impropriety. Just as He was in the garden.

Yet at the same time, in the moment He should have turned
His back on the Father for good, He does something totally
shocking. Totally unexpected. Totally . . . defiant. Do you see
the word? "Entrust." He *entrusts* Himself to His Father, even
in the most impossible of circumstances. Even when He feels
abandoned. Even in His gravestone moment. Even deeper
than the pain is something at the core of who He is that just
won't let up—*He believes His Father is good.* And so when it
makes no sense to the world, He entrusts everything to God—
His spirit, His body, this terrible moment, this disorienting
season. All of it. Instead of finding His own way through the
darkness, He gives it all to God and trusts Him. Again, just as
He did in the garden.

Jesus feels like the Father lifted His hand of favor. *But where Jesus can't feel God's hand, He trusts His Father's heart.* In the darkness and the death and the blindness, He doesn't try to analyze the situation a million different ways. He doesn't respond based on how the circumstance looks. He entrusts Himself to God in faith. Even in His dying breaths. All the way to the tomb.

And you know what? Something even more defiant happens to people who face a gravestone in faith.

They live.

Walking by Faith = Remembering

When we are right on the precipice of a spiritual breakthrough, it's easy to trust God. But when we're lost in the crisis for what feels like an endless stretch of time, it's not enticing. When we're in the dark garden, sweating drops of blood and ready to throw in the towel on this thing called Christianity, it's hard to believe this situation could be good at all. As we've seen, Jesus knows that season well. And so does the Bible. And you know how the Bible tells us to get through it? Just as Jesus did. It's called "walking by faith," a process where things like perseverance and endurance and surrender are shaped and crafted inside of us, helping us push through things like fear, doubt, anxiety, and self-reliance.

Walking by faith—what is it? How do we do it? We do it by leaning into the Father even harder than we have before, just as Jesus did. Remember: when the anguish pressed in, Jesus pressed into trust all the more fervently. As the weight got heavier, He kept releasing it, surrendering it, to His Father.

But in the darkness of it all, how do I know the Father is
someone I can trust with all that stuff? After all, the moment of
crisis is a moment of blindness. I can't see Him in those moments.
Jesus may have leaned into Him perfectly, but Jesus is divine! I'm
just little ole me! How do I lean into someone I can't see?

Great questions.

It makes sense that these kinds of questions revolve around
our ability to see and hear and feel. That's how we take in the
world, right? And so it's in gravestone seasons that we are left
looking for a sign, for grace, for the glimpse of light in a seemingly dark tomb. Our senses are in an all-out competition to
find something, anything to light our way.

When it comes to making our way through the blinding
blackness of the gravestone, the good news is that the way out
doesn't require sight. Odd, I know. But that's the Bible's brand,
right? It's counterintuitive at every turn. So here's the big
secret: "We walk by faith, not by sight." (2 Cor. 5:7). Friend,
the Bible doesn't call you to lean into trust by *seeing* but by
remembering.

Think about it. You can be in the darkest cave known to
man, or on the bottom of the ocean, or lost in the middle of
outer space, and while you can't see, you can remember all
sorts of things. Your senses may not be able to serve you, but
your *memory* can. This is why the Bible is forever telling us to
look back and remember all sorts of things. Because when we
recall all that came before us, we are given faith for right now.
So, in the darkness, when all we want to do is move forward
and *out of this place,* the counterintuitive answer for where we
should look is this: *backward.*

Remember the Ebenezers of Your Story

Isn't that a relief? You don't have to be strong enough. You don't have muster up X-ray vision to see in the dark. You don't have to be superhuman. You don't even have to conjure up the strength to take another step forward. All you have to do is look backward.

Backward at what, though? For starters, back at all the other Ebenezer stones in our journey.

If you are looking for an example of this, consider our friend David in Psalm 77. He had violence all around him, days and deeds full of injustice and hurt, all causing him to question and raise his grievances to God. He wondered if faith was even worth it. How could God be real or just when the world looks this way? When the wicked are rewarded? When the righteous are overlooked? When the deeds of other people are cutting deep and the strength is all but drained from his heart and body? When his faith is hanging by a thread? The darkness is all around him, and his faith may as well be put to death. And in his own gravestone moment, what does he look to? *What helps him make it through?*

I will remember the LORD's works. (Ps. 77:11)

Remembering his past Ebenezer moments is what got him through the deadliest season of faith and to the other side. Did you notice that it wasn't the renewed trust of others that make David feel better? It wasn't their newfound confidence in his character. It wasn't a vindicated reputation. It wasn't the opinions or deeds of other people at all. It was the deeds of the *Lord* in David's life that got him through.

But what kind of deeds? What kind of Ebenezers?

> Your path led through the sea, your way
> through the mighty waters, though your foot-
> prints were not seen. You led your people like
> a flock. (Ps. 77:19–20 NIV)

David recalled specific events woven into the story of his people and their God who made a way. He knew that the God who got His people through the Red Sea could get him through this crisis. In a present moment that should have killed his faith, the past reality of God's works helped David's faith kick in. I can imagine him now. *God has handled something bigger than this before, so I can trust Him now, even when it feels like my faith is failing me.*

Remembering the Endurance of Your Savior

When our faith is at an impasse and it's hard to hold on, the Bible gives us one more thing to look back on and remember—the work of the cross.

Remembering Christ's life and work is powerful, isn't it? After all, He's the only person in human history who faced a literal gravestone *and then walked out of it.* This is why, of all the advice in the world the Bible could give us in our own faith-feels-like-it's-failing moments, Hebrews 12 tells us to remember not just some nice principles but a person: *Jesus.* When we can't see and we're ready to throw in the towel, the writer of Hebrews says to fix our eyes on Jesus—the one who "endured" through the terror of the cross, all the way to other side of death, into resurrection life (Heb. 12:1–3). Listen to how verse 3 puts it:

> For consider him who endured such hostility
> from sinners against himself . . .

But why? Why did He endure so much when He could have just called it quits on God? On His whole mission? The rest of the verse tells us:

> . . . so that you won't grow weary and give up.

Did you catch that? Jesus endured through His doubt in the garden of Gethsemane and came out on the other side of the cross in resurrected life. He endured the darkness of that lonely garden, questioned God's ways, and then ultimately believed God. Then He went to the cross itself and even entrusted Himself and His circumstances to God there—all so you could not only have salvation *but also so that you won't grow weary and give up in your own moment of crisis.* He faced His crisis with endurance for your sake.

Look back at Him. Dear friend, look back at your Savior, who endured in His moment of darkness so that you could, too.

Jesus knew that ultimately life was on the other side of this stretch in the journey called death. The same is true for our seasons of testing and trials and doubts. The other side of the gravestone season, where our faith *should* have gone to die or deconstruct or whatever you want to call it, is resurrection. Friend, this means that the season of wrestling you are in will come around. *You'll see the other side of this.* Your faith might face its gravestone season decently intact, but while in the dark depths of the grave, it will undergo the most difficult testing you may ever experience. And yet on the other side, it will come out stronger than it was before. Radiant, tried, true, pure. When we feel battered and beat down by our season of darkness, "**let us hold on** to the confession of our hope without wavering, since he who promised is faithful" (Heb. 10:23, emphasis added). Remember: He came out on the other side of His moments of testing so that He could get you through yours. *You will make it. He will get you through this.*

Finding Our Faith

Like David and like Jesus, when we draw faith from the right well, our crisis no longer takes the place of king in our lives. We don't need a certain circumstance to go our way, hard as the situation may be, nor do we need people to believe all the right things about us. Those things don't set the temperature of our hearts or our faith anymore.

Yet it is the most difficult thing to do—to trust the Father when you're in the middle of two miracles, two Ebenezers. Isn't it? When you're in the dark and you can't see? When you're stuck like Jesus was, between two gardens. When a friend's husband leaves her for another woman, when your child loses her way, when you are drowning in a sea of depression or anger, when the business is failing, when the prayer goes unanswered, when the answer is no, when you get the terrible news of a loved one's being diagnosed with an illness. When you want to throw in the towel of "faith" altogether.

There's no sugarcoating it: the gravestone season is the hardest many of us will ever face, and we all have them. It exposes the most tender parts of our hearts, the places we've not let God touch yet. It also forces us to the fork in the road, where our faith either makes it through or we abandon Christianity as a whole.

Maybe you've also wondered if your "Jesus" season was at its death. If maybe Jesus wasn't the savior you'd actually hoped for. Perhaps you've experienced such a level of suffering and pain that the thought of God at all makes you recoil. Maybe the lack of His immediate help—or His seeming inability to intervene the way you want—makes you wonder, *Where is God in these moments?* Sometimes these trials of faith come from the hands of our choices, and others, at the hands of others. Still other times the testing comes from the hand of traveled sin. And in other situations we are tempted to walk away from God because of all the things our eyes can take in, all we can see is the rubble of a life torn apart or a life that should have been.

In these times Hebrews 11:1 reminds us of that refreshing truth we learned earlier—that faith isn't something produced by what our eyes can take in. Our trust isn't dependent on what we can see at all. "Faith is the assurance of things hoped for, the conviction of things not seen" (ESV). Assurance and hope, a conviction of *things not seen: that's* what propels us. David couldn't see past the violence all around him, but he remembered. The writer of Hebrews couldn't see past his own moment either, but he remembered Jesus—the God who endured for him in the flesh, the God he couldn't see at present but would one day see in glory. They couldn't see physically, but spiritually they looked back in just the right place to get them through.

The Greek word used most often in the New Testament for "faith" is *pistis*. It indicates a belief or conviction with the complementary idea of trust. Faith is not a mere intellectual stance but a belief that leads to action. Our belief in who God is—in His holiness and goodness—anchors and keeps us living in line with our confession. As James 2:26 says, "For as the body apart from the spirit is dead, so also faith apart from works is dead" (ESV). James talks about demonstrating his faith by his works. Often what we do says more about what we believe than what we say. Living a life of faith—a life that looks back to remember where God showed up and then walks forward in the knowledge that He'll do it again—is more important than simply speaking words of faith. We remember and then we step, even when we cannot see, trusting that at some point we will get confirmation that we are right where we need to be.

This is the life of a Christian, isn't it? We wrestle. We remember. We step. All in the dark. Because faith doesn't need sight. It can last in the dark. It can make it through the gravestone to the other side, while the world would have given up ages ago. I've said it before and I'll say it again: *we walk by faith and not by sight*. Because our sight will never be able to take us where our faith can.

You'll Come Through to the Other Side

You can have faith like this, dear friend. Like David and like Jesus and like that writer in Hebrews. You can have a faith that kicks in while you're in the dark. You can remember, like so many who have come before you, that because God has handled harder things before now, He can handle the worst of crisis moments. If He can bring His people through the Red Sea in the Old Testament, He can bring you through whatever deep water you face today.

Did you know that the Old Testament Red Sea moment is fulfilled in the New Testament? That's right. Through the death and resurrection of Jesus. Where God once delivered His people from the slavery of an Egyptian taskmaster through the waters, brought safely to the other side, He delivers us from the slavery of a taskmaster, too: sin. Jesus is the way we get delivered from our old, terrible slave master called sin and brought to the other side, safe and sound. We are delivered just as God's people were.

What does this mean for us in our gravestone moments of doubt? It means that if the Father can get His people through the waters to free them from slavery, and He can also see Jesus through to the other side of His death, and He can also deliver you from your sin and bring you safely back into relationship with Him forever, then *He can get you and me through any crisis.* Even the "close to giving up my faith" kind of crisis. Yes He can. He's made a way before. He'll make a way again. He's handled the Red Sea. Deliverance was on the other side. He's handled the cross. Resurrection was on the other side. He can handle your gravestone moment. *And He'll give you newness of life and strength of faith on the other side of it.*

So, what does holding on in the dark sound like while we wait for the deliverance? As the intensity of the gravestone season presses up against us, what will hold us up so that we don't fall down? As we said before, our remembrance of Christ and our Ebenezer moments. The ones we've been charting all the way through this book! They are there, in black and white as you've written them down, for such a time as this. They exist for you to be able to look back and say along with David: "I will remember the LORD's works!" They exist for you to declare in the dark: *I see the way His hand has shown up in the past, even when I thought it couldn't. And so it must be true now, too. Even when Your footprints aren't seen in this tomb, God, in this dead place where my faith feels like it's failing, You've made a way before and I believe against all odds You'll do it again. I can't see, but I remember. You're the God who delivered Your people from slavery in Egypt—You made a way. You're the God who delivered me from sin—You made a way. You're the God who raised Your Son and delivered Him from the dead—You made a way. I lift my eyes to these things, even now. Even in the dark. I look up to the stones you've erected before now, I list them all out before You—I remember each one. And I believe You can build a new one here, even in this grave I feel like I'm in. Because You're the God who moves not just mountains but tombstones.*

Friend, that's what belief sounds like in the dark. When our faith feels like it met its death and we can't see our next Ebenezer stone, we walk by faith in the dark, lifting our eyes to the endurance of Jesus and our past Ebenezer stones, remembering God as faithful. The next stone will come. God's hand will move. He has proven true before. He'll do it again. Even in a tomb. Especially in a tomb. We can trust His heart. Because crisis has nothing on God. If He can resurrect a dead Son, He can resurrect a dying faith. Hear it again: *He can resurrect when your faith lies in its grave.* Yes, even there.

Can I make a suggestion? Invite your soul back to this place of remembrance when it seems to forget. Tell your heart and mind to come and recall the goodness of God, the love, the mercy, the way He's already gone before you. Jesus gifts you perseverance and endurance because of the work on the cross. I think Jesus invites us into something beautiful here—endurance that isn't produced so much by the specifics of what we go through but more so on how much we are willing to depend on Him. Even when we can see, walking by sight will disorient us and leave us disillusioned. So He gives us a better way, a better choice, a clearer path in walking by faith—because it will lead us back not only to the truth but onward to the plans He has for us.

More Than a Feeling

One of the things I love about my kids is that our bond goes deeper than most human relationships. Friends come and go. Neighbors move away. If you don't feel like answering a random text from an acquaintance, it's not the end of the world because acquaintances are transient. Who knows if they'll be there tomorrow. But my kids? It doesn't really matter how I feel on a random Tuesday morning—the sun will come up and we're all going to need breakfast and lunches packed and kisses as we exit the home and enter our world of school or work or church. Nor does my mood factor into the equation when they text me for a ride from school. I'm going to be there to pick them up, bad mood or good, good circumstances or bad. Why? *Because I'm their mom.* They're family. They're flesh and blood. Feelings are important, no doubt. And we have to hash through them together. But at the end of the day, what binds us isn't how we feel. We're in this life together, for good, no matter what the circumstances look like.

You know what proves that me and my kid are actually family and not some other random type of relationship? The morning after a big disagreement. I know, it's odd to say. But those are the best mornings. Because we can drive each other crazy on Monday, and even go to sleep frustrated sometimes, and then wake up the next day, walk out of our rooms, and show up to the family table. We're all still there, each person accounted for. The relationships were tested and tried, and yet the morning comes and we're all still together. Now we may need to have a chat and some reconciliation moments about whatever happened the day before. *But we're all there to do it.* No matter what Monday held, we show up on Tuesday. We make it to the other side of the situation, and our relationship proves true. Durable. Lasting. Perseverant.

That's family.

Sometimes you and I have to remind ourselves what category our relationship with God goes in. Sometimes we need to remember that it's not in the friends or neighbors or acquaintances category. It's in the family category. The *forever, in it for good,* category. Our faith in our Lord—it's more than a feeling. It's a resolve. It's living from the conviction that God is who He says He is, even when our feelings say otherwise. Even when we're just shy of the next miracle. It's the perseverance of faith produced in crises and seasons of wilderness that serves as a signpost of the power and glory of God. A faith tested, tried, and found true on the other side. This is what He wants for us, a faith unmoved by the lack of what we see, or the temporary confusion of whatever the current situation looks like, but fueled by what we know to be eternally true in Christ Jesus, the one who reconciled us to the Father. A faith based not on what we see but on what we know. This gravestone moment in our faith is just a Monday in light of eternity, and tomorrow will be here in the blink of an eye, when we dine with our Father at the table forever.

We can endure what's in front of us when we live in this sort of perspective, am I right? The gravestone season is real and it's hard—don't get me wrong. It will deeply test what category we put God in. But if we're truly His, *it's also just a Monday.* And He will see us through it. He will be there tomorrow, on the other side of all this doubt and struggle and darkness, waiting to meet us. Because He's our Father. He's family. Feelings and moods aside, even if we're between two miracles and we can't see, we can be assured: He will show up. He will always show up.

Marked by Faith

Gravestones usually have some sort of marking on them: a name, date of birth, and also the day of passing. Sometimes you will also find notes or messages engraved on the headstone. More often than not they are there to remind visitors that there was once life where this gravestone now stands. These messages remind visitors to look back and delight themselves in the memories of what once was, in hopes that this moment will give them enough joy, enough strength, enough healing, to keep going.

And I think the same is true for our "gravestone" seasons—the ones where our faith faces the threat of death, of extinction. The ones where we are tempted to throw our walk with God into a coffin and bury it for good—tempted to just hang up our "Jesus season" and go at life alone without Him. Once God brings us through that terrifying moment where we're sure our faith won't make it another day and helps us to the other side, we find that, if we look closely, there are markings left in that place. We find that though that season of total blindness carries scars, it is also marked as our greatest moment of faith. And somehow the gravestone even becomes yet another Ebenezer stone in our story to look back on, seeing how God got us this far once again.

My faith should have stayed in the grave on that date night with Mario. Instead, God resurrected my faith and my marriage. I supposed I shouldn't be surprised. God's greatest work always happens at grave sites. And now that tombstone reads: "Here should lie Alexandra's faith. But it is not here. It is risen." Now, when I look back, I can see where we were standing: Mario and I were in the middle of a miracle. God put broken pieces of our battered faith back together and bound us up with His grace. The next Ebenezer wasn't so far away. It was just on the other side of the darkness. And God brought us through.

That can be your story, too, no matter how close to death your faith feels. We *do* come to the other side of this crisis; *you* do, my dear friend. Hope and faith will pull you out of the gravestone, right back onto the living Stone, Jesus Christ. Something in us, holy and divine, beckons us to keep going. Although right now you may only see the darkness and feel the cold of the tomb your faith is facing, you may not realize that you're standing just a few feet away from the stone that has been rolled away as a door for you to walk through. You may not know just how close you are to the other side of this trial. You can't see. But Jesus can. He knows what the grave feels like, and He knows how to walk you through the moment it feels like your faith is on its last breath. And you know what? Jesus tells us a different story while we face the darkness: one of victory and grace.

What situation in your life right now makes you want to walk away from God? Whatever it is, whatever you're walking through, it may feel like it's leading you to a total deconstruction. But in this "gravestone" moment, when faced with the choice, we can believe God in the death and in the dark. Because God's a better leader than that thing, right? He leads us to better places—He leads His people to *life*. When life throws your belief system in a coffin and threatens to *hammer in the nails to call it quits on this thing called following Jesus, let me remind you: we have something we can look to in the dark.* We can remember the endurance of our Savior. And we can fall back on our Ebenezer stones, lifting our eyes to remember all the places He's met us before now. We can remember that God's hand was always at work in so many seasons before now, and it is still at work right now.

Looking Up

If your faith is at that crossroads right now, friend, hold on to the hand of the Shepherd who knows how to lead you through what seems like the death of your faith, and He has the power to resurrect it. After all, if the Father can raise His Son from the dead, He can raise your faith. If He does His best work on literal tombs, He can do it in the tomb it feels like your faith is trapped in. Lift your eyes, even in the dark and the cold and the lifelessness of it all.

Say it to yourself. Remember. *Your God makes a way. Your God brings life to death. Your God parts the waters. Your God rescues, delivers, restores. Your God doesn't deconstruct you; He builds you up. Your God has shown up before. Your God can do it again.* That's the kind of Father He is. Like Jesus, *entrust* yourself to Him in this moment. Hand Him the faith that feels like it's on its last breath, and watch Him breathe life into it. Remember the times He's done that for you before. Exhale all that pent-up doubt, entrusting it to Him, and believe He can give you fresh wind and fresh fire. Cry out to Him from your gravestone moment, from your place of blindness, and before long you'll *see.* You'll see you were standing in the middle of a miracle. The crisis was real, yes. But it had nothing on God. It had zero chance to stop His faithful love from bringing you to the other side of the stormy sea. It became its own Ebenezer moment that you can mark in your story and lift your eyes to in future moments of struggle—a place where God really did show up and save you.

Just like He's done before.

Just like He'll do again.

EYES UP

Lift your eyes and look back on your own journey, taking the time to chart this crucial moment (or season) in your life.

1. Are you currently facing a season of spiritual doubt, where your faith feels like its hanging by a thread or facing its death? If not, have you ever faced that kind of season in your past? What caused it?

2. How did God meet you in this season, and how did He bring you through to the other side? (If you are currently in this season, what are some evidences that He is in the darkness with you?)

3. In this chapter, we explored Luke 22:42–44; 2 Corinthians 5:7; and Hebrews 11:1; 12:2–3. Read the passages again and consider these questions:

- What about these passages helps you in your gravestone season?
- What is surprising or unexpected about these passages?
- How have you seen them prove true in your life?

4. In this chapter we explored two things to remember in a gravestone season: the endurance of your Savior and the Ebenezers in your story. Which of these two things is hardest to remember for you? How might you take steps to help yourself remember them in the future?

7 | The Stone of Surrender
God's Will over My Way

I don't think you're equipped enough for the role.

We've decided to give it to someone else.

We're going another direction.

Maybe you've heard some version of these statements before. And if you're anything like me, it's not really the wording that leaves a lasting impression or the specific job or role you wanted. What lingers is the emotional blow that comes with a loud and clear *no*.

I'd worked in small-group ministry for years, first as a ministry assistant and then as a coordinator. After some difficult transitions that left roles open and our group leaders rattled, it made sense that they were looking for consistency and shepherding. They wanted a leader they knew and trusted. And I just knew the person they needed was me. Not because I was somebody special but because they knew me. They trusted

me. More than that, I knew them and loved them and really
desired to take care of them during a tough time.

In my heart I just knew my time had finally come to step
into the position God had called me to do. With a knot in my
stomach and shaking knees, I knew I had to have the conversation. I needed to admit to both myself and my then leader that
this was the direction and position I believed God was leading
me to do. I'd spent years faithfully serving, years of showing
up early and leaving late. Years giving of myself not just in fun
spaces but in spaces where my worth and value were unseen, or
even undermined at times. It had to be time. Right?

My mother-in-law has told me this for years: "It may not
be on *my* time, but God is always on time." I would always roll
my eyes when I heard that. But now, in this season of ministry, with this job I knew was supposed to pan out, it was true.
Although God may not work on our time, He is never late.

See, this job I thought I was clearly the right fit for—well,
it wasn't my time for it. Or, as my mom-in-law would say, it
wasn't on my time.

"We've chosen to go in a different direction, someone with
a different skill set."

The words brought back a world of familiar pain—rejection. Not just a closed door but one locked with dead bolts.
One I so desperately wanted to pull open with my own bare
hands.

How could the answer be rejection? How could the answer
just be *no*? I was so sure this was God's call. I knew it was a
God dream. But I guess it was someone else's, too. And you
know what? This wasn't the only no I would encounter. There
would be many around the bend. In fact, God has gifted me

more noes than I can count over the last fourteen years of my life, and I'm sure there are more to come. Noes to prayers, noes to dreams that were, in my mind, supposed to be Ebenezer stones He showed up for and marked in my story.

I couldn't see it at the time, but through the journey of no after no, I learned something—that what the world knows as rejection, Christians know as something else.

But now I'm getting ahead of myself.

Forcing God's Hand

I remember the first time my oldest daughter Leilla tried to force something out of my hands. She desperately wanted a toy I had taken from her. She had to have been around three years old, a spicy little thing with the strength of a girl who will one day leave the people around her knowing God more because of it. No matter what type of parenting tool or trick we tried, she'd find a way to remind us that she wanted her way, and anything other than a "here you go" or "yes" was not going to cut it.

We'd sit her down and remind her that there was a reason mommy and daddy had chosen to take the toy. But she didn't want an explanation—just the toy. And she made sure we knew it.

Whether it was time for bed, time for dinner, there was always a reason, and a good reason at that, to take the toy away. It was never done out of ill intent, never just because we felt like it. *Taking the toy at the right time was actually always for her good.* But at this point in her life, she couldn't see the whole picture. She didn't understand, and it was our job to guide her in a way that would give her the best outcome at that very moment, to protect and love her well.

And from that love, that flowed these guardrails of grace, I wish I could've explained to her all the ways this seemingly small moment could impact her overall well-being and health. I wish I could have made her understand that her little body needed a break from all the stimulation and that a good plate of dinner and family time were just what she needed. That toy would be there later, and even if it wasn't, new yeses would come her way at exactly the time they'd be good for her.

We treat so many things like that toy, don't we? We see something we want so bad in the hands of God—a position, a husband, a child, a job, a house, a certain amount of influence, or a certain number in the bank account to make us feel okay inside. And we can't, for the life of us, understand why He would say no. We want that Ebenezer story so bad we can taste it.

"Look how God showed up! I got the job!"

"The Lord met me in that place of loneliness, and He met me with a man!'

"I raise my Ebenezer right here. God brought the money, and now we have the house and the fence and the two-car garage!"

And I'm sure God does build those Ebenezers in the lives of certain people. But what if His answer in the place you want Him to build it for *you* is *no*? What do you do?

If you're anything like me, sometimes you try to steal it back. You try to make it happen. You try to force His hand to move, prying His fingers open until you can reach the gift inside. Like Leilla, no just isn't cutting it, so you come up with some plan to build an Ebenezer in a place God never intended to build one because He had other plans. You try to make a good thing a God thing even when God's not in it.

But thankfully, God knows the difference between a good thing and a God thing, between what we want and what we need. And He builds Ebenezers in exactly the way He wants to. His hand cannot be forced. And while that drives us crazy in some seasons, when we get to the other side of the struggle, we realize this is actually the best news in the world. Where the kings of this world can be manipulated, God can't.

A King that Doesn't Get His Way

Speaking of kings, there's a story in 1 Kings 22 that recently caught my attention. As we read, we find ourselves caught in-between a man's way and God's will. The king of Israel is determined to take back some land that once belonged to his people, a land called Ramoth Gilead.

To that end, the king of Israel asks the king of Judah for help. Together, if they join forces and combine their militaries, they have a real shot at winning. The king of Judah agrees that this could be a good idea but wisely responds by saying, "First, please ask what the LORD's will is" (1 Kings 22:5).

So how does one figure out God's will back in those days? Prophets. True prophets tell the truth; they only speak what God has genuinely revealed to them. They carry the word of the Lord. False prophets do the opposite; they speak for God in whatever way they want, even when God hasn't actually spoken on a matter. They speak *as if* they carry the word of the Lord, but eventually things don't go as they said it would, and they prove themselves false.

So, as the story goes, the king of Israel agrees to stop and inquire about God's will (win!), but he does so through by a bunch of false prophets (fail!). He surrounds himself with those who will tell him what he wants to hear. The false prophets all tell him the same thing. Here's how it goes down:

> The king of Israel got the prophets together—all four hundred of them—and put the question to them: "Should I attack Ramoth Gilead? Or should I hold back?"
>
> "Go for it," they said. "GOD will hand [the victory and the land] over to the king."
> (1 Kings 22:6 MSG)

The king of Judah feels like something is off and asks if there are any true prophets nearby—perhaps one who doesn't always say what people want to hear but rather communicates what *God* thinks. Thankfully, there is one such prophet. His name is Micaiah.

Even with a million other voices telling the king that God will pull through for Israel in this battle, Micaiah pronounces the opposite. He tells the truth and makes clear that if the king of Israel chooses to go into this battle, he won't return from it, and his people will scatter because their leader has perished (1 Kings 22:17). In doing this, Micaiah challenges the assumption that this Ebenezer is a given. *You're not going to get the victory this way, king. If you try to force this, it won't go well for you.*

What happens? Well, the king of Israel wants this win so bad that he does not listen to God's true prophet. He only listens to the voices who agree with him and tell him his desired outcome. How sad. The will of God is made plain as day as God tries to warn the king through Micaiah. Yet the king is so set on this "Ebenezer" happening, so sure the Lord will meet them and hand them the victory, that he strikes out on his own and chooses to go into battle anyway. And just as God said, Israel loses and the king himself dies.

A Choice We Have to Make

In a moment Israel really wanted God to show up for them in a certain way, God's answer was no. Though He had shown up many times in battle for His people and given them such amazing Ebenezers in their military history, this wasn't one of those times. He had not chosen to build this Ebenezer, and He tried to tell them so. He told them not to walk outside of His will, and their king led them to do just that. The king did not like the way God's hand was moving, so he tried to force it to move in some other direction.

But God won't build an Ebenezer stone He isn't interested in building. See, one of the gifts we find in God's character is His moral purity and His total control over the world. He knows what is right, and He cannot be forced or persuaded or coaxed to do anything outside of His will. He's not a puppet and He cannot be manipulated or corrupted. His arm cannot be twisted to do something that is not in His good plan. His will goes. Not ours. He builds the Ebenezers He wants to build, and we cannot make Him build otherwise. And when we sense the temptation to step around His plans or force His hand, we have the choice to continue down that path or surrender to God's will. We can choose God's good will over our way.

I think the king of Israel desperately wanted a way out of God's will, overlooking the Father's kind warning to follow his own desires. I believe doubt, pride, and fear led him to create a contingency plan of sorts, a way to follow his own way over God's will just in case the word of God was wrong.

Thing is, we can be a lot like that king, can't we? *We have some stones to build, yes,* but we can sometimes strike out on our own and build the wrong ones—ones God never told us to build, on paths He never told us to go down. We try to erect stones God didn't help us with, towers of Babel, paths built up from fear and the need to control. They aren't authentic Ebenezer stones but fabricated mile markers in our life, ones we are trying to force God's hand to build—a lousy relationship we insist on pursuing, a job we shouldn't take, a house we shouldn't buy right now. Trying with all our might to will our way into something or, other times, out of it, believing that our God can be maneuvered into giving us some shiny "toy" we think is best.

And when we find we cannot force Him to bless us in some way, or show up and build some Ebenezer we desperately want, we take Him out of the equation and take the seat of god ourselves. We think, *If God is not good to me, then I will make sure to be good to myself.* In these ways and more, like the king, we reach for control and power, and we don't realize that we're being led into confusion and chaos.

But friend, it doesn't have to be that way. We have a choice. Fear tells us we know better; faith says God's way is better. We can choose the way of faith. We don't have to build something God isn't in, only to see it fall. We don't have to be like the king of Israel, elbowing our way to a miracle God never meant to give us, only to get to it and find ash in our hands in the very place we thought there would be blessing. We can choose the way of the other king—the king of Judah—who stops and says, *"Wait, let's ask what the Lord's will is."*

God's Will

God's will has always been hard for me to understand. What is it? Can I trust it? In the seasons of life when it's hard to wait on God or take the time to discern God's will, we typically strive and make our way in haste. His will becomes an afterthought and not our guide. So, what is His will? And how do we follow it?

Romans 12:2 offers so much help as we seek to answer these questions:

> Do not conform to the pattern of this world, but be transformed by the renewing of your mind. Then you will be able to test and approve what God's will is—his good, pleasing and perfect will. (NIV)

Good and pleasing and perfect. Those are the first things we can know about God's will. It's not bad, it's not lacking pleasure, and it's not flawed. God's will means God's desires and His plans in this world. And when we read Romans 12:1–2, we see that those desires and plans can be trusted.

And how do we discern such a good, pleasing, and perfect will? With a transformed, renewed mind. A renewed mind helps us know the difference when we are looking at a pattern of the world versus when we are looking at the path of God. Or, said another way, as our mind is renewed according to the things of God, we can then better discern and know God's perfect will.

With a renewed mind, we can love God, become more like God, and love God's people. We can live in a Mark 12:30–31 and Matthew 6:10 way, bringing heaven to earth.

With a renewed mind, we can trust God as He leads us, even when we cannot see it or feel it. We can lean into His heart and desires as guardrails, moving in step with where He says to go, and at what pace He desires us to take, just as Christ did, for we are given the mind of Christ (1 Cor. 2:16).

So the obvious next question becomes, *How do we get a renewed mind?* Or said another way, *What, exactly, renews our mind in this way,* so that we can identify a pattern of the world and walk in step with God's desire for us instead?

I love how simply the Bible answers this: "Understanding your word brings light to the minds of ordinary people" (Ps. 119:130 CEV). God's Word! As we immerse ourselves in Scripture, letting it pierce us to the deepest levels by the power of the Holy Spirit, it will start reshaping and renewing our mind. Or, put more simply, the world might talk to us to try to convince us of its ways, but God talks to us, too, through His Word. So, if we turn from listening to the world and choose to listen to Him in His Word, we will be convinced of *His* ways instead. In obeying His Word and relying on His Spirit, we find that we are given the mind of Christ more and more.

If God's will still seems murky to you, be encouraged. Because the Word of God demystifies it. In so many places in Scripture, God has clearly laid out His general will for us all. Let's explore some of these places together.

Consider what Jesus says in John 6:38–40 about God's will:

> For I have come down from heaven, not to do my own will, but the will of him who sent me. **This is the will of him who sent me:** that I should lose none of those he has given me but should raise them up on the last day. For **this is the will of my Father:** that everyone who sees the Son and believes in him will have eternal life, and I will raise him up on the last day. (emphasis added)

Want to know the Father's will? His will is for Jesus to never lose you now that you're His. His will is to raise you up in resurrection power on the last day. His will for you is to be saved, sanctified, and glorified through Christ Jesus.

Or consider Ephesians 5:15–21:

> Pay careful attention, then, to how you walk— not as unwise people but as wise—making the most of the time, because the days are evil. So don't be foolish, but **understand what the Lord's will is**. And don't get drunk with wine, which leads to reckless living, but be filled by the Spirit: speaking to one another in psalms, hymns, and spiritual songs, singing

and making music with your heart to the
Lord, giving thanks always for everything to
God the Father in the name of our Lord Jesus
Christ, submitting to one another in the fear
of Christ. (emphasis added)

Want to know what God's will is? For you to walk in
wisdom, be filled with His Spirit, continue showing up for
your covenant community, and live in a way that gives thanks.
That's God's will for your life.

How about 1 Peter 2:15? What does that tell us about
God's will?

For **it is God's will** that you silence the
ignorance of foolish people by doing good.
(emphasis added)

If we're wondering about God's will for our lives this week,
Peter says it's this right here. To silence any foolishness around
us not with cleverness or anger but by doing good! Friend,
God's will for your life is to be His image bearer, living out
your faith in love and action. *Good works* are His will for you.

And while we're in Peter's neighborhood, let's not forget
1 Peter 4:19:

So then, let those who **suffer according to
God's will** entrust themselves to a faithful
Creator while doing what is good. (emphasis
added)

This tells us that sometimes God's will isn't always rain-
bows and butterflies. I mean, it certainly wasn't for Jesus on

the week He was betrayed and went to the cross! Peter teaches us that we may experience difficult times as a part of God's will, and in that, God calls us to entrust our souls to Him, our faithful and trustworthy Creator. This is a declaration to ourselves, and to the world around us, that we will not wait for circumstances to improve before we call God good. This is a reminder that sometimes God's will includes a cross to bear, and even when that happens, we will believe that our good God is caring for us through our suffering and into the glory of eternity.

Okay just one more. Let's consider 1 Thessalonians 5:12–18:

> Now we ask you, brothers and sisters, to give recognition to those who labor among you and lead you in the Lord and admonish you, and to regard them very highly in love because of their work. Be at peace among yourselves. And we exhort you, brothers and sisters: warn those who are idle, comfort the discouraged, help the weak, be patient with everyone. See to it that no one repays evil for evil to anyone, but always pursue what is good for one another and for all. Rejoice always, pray constantly, give thanks in everything; for **this is God's will for you** in Christ Jesus. (emphasis added)

Here we see exactly what God's will is for us. It is fleshed out when we honor and recognize one another, encourage one another, support one another, be peacemakers, comfort the hurting, warn those who are idle, exhibit patience, pursue what is always good for those around us, rejoice in God, pray consistently, and practice gratitude.

Have you noticed anything in our tour-de-verses about God's will? I have—it's that God's will is not hidden behind some curtain for only the super-spiritual Christians to figure out! His general will for every single one of us is revealed in black and white, right there in His Word. We don't have to worry about missing it; He's made so much of it clear, and put it right in front of us.

But What about the Specific Situations?

"Okay, Alexandra, I get all that general stuff about God's overall desires and purposes for His people, including me. But what about specific situations I need clarity on? The stuff God's Word doesn't speak directly about?"

Great question. Can I start by making one observation? We often overlook God's instructed will—the stuff He's made clear in His Word that we explored before—and become overly focused and consumed with the unknown. We want to know God's hidden will for the future while walking contrary to His revealed will in the Scripture and in the present. Is this true for you? I know it's been true for me at various points! Before we head down the road of discerning God's specific will in certain situations, let's stop and ask if we're actually obeying all the stuff He's already made clear. Because when we are, we're far more likely to hear Him on the specific stuff.

I'll say it this way: following God's revealed will for us means we are to love God, be transformed into the likeness of Jesus, stay faithful to our covenant community, and love our neighbors. If we do this, it turns us into the sort of person who can discern the specific will of God within complicated situations. As we love God completely, ourselves correctly, our brothers and sisters consistently, and our neighbors compassionately, we become people who don't have to try so hard to "hear" God. Our instincts will be increasingly more like His, so that when specific things happen, and complications arise, our knee-jerk reactions and ways of considering solutions are more in line with God's heart and God's ways than they were just years before. As we sit under good preaching and teaching, as we read and study and memorize our Bibles in a covenant community, we will grow in our ability to know God's will. We will become more discerning people. And as we renew our minds, the Spirit of God will help us not only discern God's will (Rom. 12:2) but also apply it to the circumstances and moments of our days.

So, if you're wondering what to do with something specific in your life—whom you should marry, if you should take the job, what boundaries look like in a certain relationship, etc.— let me encourage you to immerse yourself in God's Word, lean into solid Christian counsel, pray often, and listen for the Holy Spirit's guidance. I can't tell you exactly what you should do, but I do know that a person who prioritizes these things is far more discerning in crucial moments than a person who does not.

What if I'm Outside of God's Will?

I'll ask this question both to you and to myself: Where are we outside of God's revealed will? Or, perhaps I'll ask it this way: Where are we obsessed with finding God's hidden will about some specific situation when we are walking contrary to His already-revealed will in the Bible? Look back up at the Scripture passages above, and take some time to consider this question in honesty—not before me but before God and yourself, just the two of you.

Here's an example: Let's say Sally is on social media today, asking for prayer. She needs God to reveal which direction she should go in a certain relationship or with a certain job. "Join me in praying, friends. Ask God to reveal His will for me in this situation! Please God, build an Ebenezer in this place! I know You'll show up!" Naturally, we stop and pray for Sally. But then let's say we scroll down and see that her social media feed, right underneath her prayer request, is full of sarcastic memes and cutting remarks, aimed at those she disagrees with. She makes fun of them. She laughs at their expense. She is ruthless toward those she considers fools, whether that's a political party or a theological tribe or someone on the other side of a particular culture war. She is clearly trusting in the world's way of doing battle. Here we see that Sally wants God's specific will, but she's not willing to walk in line with His already revealed will as seen in the Bible, where Sally is told to silence fools not by lashing out but by doing good.

How are you and I like Sally today? In what places are we so obsessed with the *unknown* will of God in some particular situation that we don't even realize we've stepped out of His *known* will for us? Said in a broader way, where are our lives not squaring with Scripture?

Being out of God's will is being in direct opposition to God's desire for us as seen in His Word. This means that we step outside of God's will when we step outside of the Bible's call to love Him, walk in His ways, and become more like Jesus—it's that simple. We are outside of His will any time we are not doing those things.

Don't worry though. If you're thinking, as I often do, *There are so many places I'm not making the mark and living according to Scripture,* hear some warm encouragement: there's grace even in this. Remember, God's will for us is to become like Jesus and embody His vision and mission on this side of heaven. And that sanctification process is a slow one where we change in small degrees over time. We will miss the mark sometimes. We will stray from God's revealed will in certain moments. But when we do, there's a way to step back on the right path. Scripture calls this step *repentance.*

Repentance means to turn away from something and move toward something else. It's the acknowledgment of our miss, and it is our active participation with the Holy Spirit's power and conviction to turn around, back toward loving God with our whole hearts. It realigns us with God's will for our lives, which is living in alignment with His Word and His ways. And repentance shouldn't only happen a couple of times in our lives. We should have a lifestyle of repentance. This proves that we are choosing God's will and God's ways over our own on a consistent basis.

Repentance isn't complicated—it's just another word for *surrender.* It's when we stop trying to build some "Ebenezer" God never intended for us and step back into God's will.

Surrender and a Better Yes

If you're looking for a biblical example of this, consider Moses. I can relate more to Moses than I care to admit.

If anyone deserved a big Ebenezer moment in life, it was Moses, right? He had endured the grumbling of the people and the years and years of walking around in circles. He had brought them safely through their exodus and given the law to them so they'd know how to live in the land of promise. And finally, when it seemed to be the perfect time for God to pull through for him, when the season came to actually cross over into the promised land, . . . *Moses didn't get to go in.*

In the first chapter of Deuteronomy, we learn that God tells Moses that he's not the one who will lead the Israelites into the promised land. Instead, they'll be led by a new leader, Joshua, and Moses will not enter with them (1:37–40). There Moses has it: God's will made clear, plain as day. A few chapters go by, though, and we find that Moses is clearly not liking what God has revealed. Like a lot of us, Moses tries to change God's mind and begs Him for the Ebenezer moment he always thought he'd get:

> At that same time, I begged GOD: "GOD, my
> Master, you let me in on the beginnings, you
> let me see your greatness, you let me see your
> might—what god in Heaven or Earth can do
> anything like what you've done! Please, let me
> in also on the endings, let me cross the river
> and see the good land over the Jordan, the
> lush hills, the Lebanon mountains." (Deut.
> 3:23–25 MSG)

Although Moses tries to flatter God with eloquence, God sticks to His own will on the matter.

> But GOD was still angry with me because of you. He wouldn't listen. He said, "Enough of that. Not another word from you on this. Climb to the top of Mount Pisgah and look around: look west, north, south, east. Take in the land with your own eyes. Take a good look because you're not going to cross this Jordan.
>
> "Then command Joshua: Give him courage. Give him strength. Single-handed he will lead this people across the river. Single-handed he'll cause them to inherit the land at which you can only look." (Deut. 3:26–28 MSG)

What? This was Moses's big moment. This was what all the work was for! This was his God dream. By everyone's earthly understanding and logic, *this was supposed to be an Ebenezer God built in Moses's life.* Except the hard truth is this: it wasn't. God wasn't going to come through in this particular way at this particular time. What Moses wanted wasn't ultimately what God wanted, no matter how much Moses tried to twist His arm. God had assigned Moses to be the leader the people needed at the beginning of this particular season in their history and Joshua to be the leader in the next season. That was God's revealed will, and no amount of flattery was going to change it.

Friend, this has been a hard lesson for me to learn, but it's a true one: God builds the Ebenezers *He* wants to build in order to write the story *He* wants to write. He gets to decide the characters and the seasons and the way things go down. Because He's God. And we are not.

This doesn't mean He's not compassionate to our cries. And it doesn't mean He isn't kind. It means He's the one in control. He's the heavenly Parent. And like me and Leilla with the toy, the parent gets to decide when to say no, or when to take something away, for our good.

Though Moses pleaded and tried to work around God's revealed will, God's purposes stayed the same. And finally, if we flip all the way to Deuteronomy 32, we see that Moses surrendered to God's will, climbed the mountain God told him to climb so that he might look at the land, and then he died there.

Though Moses didn't get to enter the promised land in his earthly life as we'd all hoped for him to, the takeaway is that he eventually surrendered to God's plan instead of his own. He gave up the pleading match and trusted God, ending up exactly where God wanted him to end up. God is a way maker, even when we see no way out, or even through.

God does something remarkable, though, for Moses. He honors his obedience and life, and we see a miraculous appearance of Moses again in the New Testament on the Mount of Transfiguration, where he gets to talk to Jesus from beyond the grave. From up on that mountain, He could see the promise. Jesus Christ was the fulfilment of all the promises in the Old Testament, and here is Moses, staring that Promise in the face! As it turns out, God wanted Moses to see something, or rather, *someone*, that was even better than the land he loved and labored for.

Amazing. God is not tied to our planning but to His divine timing. His will is better than our own every time.

Moses never could have known he'd see the true fulfillment of all he had worked so hard for. But that was God's eventual will for him—to meet Christ himself on a mountain. Moses was told no in ways he'd never gets answers for in his earthly life. His request was rejected. And that's a hard pill to swallow—not just for Moses but for you and me. Sometimes we don't get to know the reason the answer was no. Sometimes we don't get a heavenly explanation for why a certain Ebenezer was never in God's plan to build.

But beyond the grave, we see that what felt like rejection for Moses in the moment was really just divine redirection. God had a plan in store for Moses that traveled down different paths than he could have ever imagined. Beyond the grave, Moses got to understand the why, and he got to encounter Christ. That was God's will for him, and he surrendered to it in the moment he didn't understand, only to fully understand on the other side of eternity. Only to fully enjoy what all the good gifts point to anyway: Jesus.

You and I will one day get to see this grace, too. We will understand how rejections were really divine redirections. Maybe now, hopefully now, but if not—when we do, we will see an even greater understanding of this wild thing called life and all the yeses and noes that come with it. Better yet, we will get to see God's hand at work from that bird's-eye view. And ultimately, we'll get to see how Jesus was the answer and the promise and the Ebenezer we'd been hoping for all along.

For our friend Moses, surrender meant stepping into alignment with what God wanted to do instead of fighting for his own way. It meant stopping and believing that God is better at being in control than he was. For Moses and for us, it means letting God be God, which looks like letting go of any dearly held Ebenezer dreams if God makes clear He doesn't want to build them, trusting that somehow there's a better yes in Jesus.

Giving God the Desires

So, where does that leave our dreams and desires? The ones that are good and helpful? After all, Moses himself wanted a good thing, not a bad thing. When we submit our desires and will to the Father, our good desires are not put out but surrendered to the Father's better way. They are handed over to the Potter's hand to shape and mold the clay we so desperately have been trying to mold ourselves. Even the most tender places of our hearts are safe with Him. And when the clay meets the Potter, when our heart meets His hand, when our lives meet His heart, He begins to reshape and mold, chipping away at our doubt with grace and love. In the surrender process, He may not give us the thing we want. He may not make the circumstance different exactly when or how we want Him to. But He makes *us* different. He turns us into a vessel of faith instead of a vessel of anger and bitterness and resentment. He molds us into a person who can lift her eyes instead of hanging her head. He transforms us into a person who can believe, despite all odds, that He is good and that He is good to us.

I don't want to live in the fear that God may not be who He says He is. I don't want to live a life in bondage to my control and thoughts when freedom to live in God's peace and grace is inviting me in. If it's His will over my way, then my need to surrender must supersede my desire to control. And the good news is that I can. I *can* surrender through the help of the Holy Spirit, through the strength of the cross, and through the power of the empty tomb. I can land in the place of faith that rejections in this life are being used by God as holy redirections.

Life may not change around me, my circumstances may stay the same, and my heart will still be filled with dreams and prayers of what could be, but my desire to know God and follow His will leads me in them and through them. My need to control will flee when I know I can trust the One who is in control—safely handing over my heart to the One who can tend to it best, make me different, and remind me that *I already have* the truest and best promise of the world—Jesus.

As we surrender whatever Ebenezer we were hoping God might build, we get to behold on the God *behind* the Ebenezer, finally fixing our eyes on our Savior Himself instead of the stuff we hoped He might give us. As we lay down our will, we step into alignment with His.

So, what does stepping into alignment with God's will look like for you and for me, practically speaking? We know the answer is "surrender," but what does it look like to surrender the Ebenezers we have in mind so that we might let God build the ones He's written in His own plan for us?

Just Turn Around

Let me stop right here and encourage you before we go any farther: the Father isn't after some long, drawn-out fight with you. He's not chasing down all the things you care about and forcefully taking them away just to mess with you. No, your willingness and posture in trusting the Father is what He's after. God will not strong-arm us to surrender or trust. Rather, He'll patiently and lovingly wait until we sit at His feet, humbly surrendering the ways that we've kept clenched up in our fists for far too long. And it's there when we make room to release the way we once followed, where we turn back to God. This is what surrender and repentance really look like. It is to stop the direction we were headed, turn around, look up, back up, and walk His direction in a practical way. It's not just a sorrowful feeling that happens in the heart, though godly sorrow is important. Getting back in line means actually moving your feet in another direction.

I think about Sally. What does getting back into God's will look like for her? What do surrender and repentance mean? It doesn't just mean feeling bad for the way she handled her social media account. It means actually changing the way she handles it from now on. It means godly speech online in the place where ungodly words once lived, and more than that, it means silencing fools with good works instead of harsh words.

What might it look like for you and me to release our will to God's? To surrender that Ebenezer to Him that He might be saying no to? In some seasons it might look like waiting instead of actively pursuing something or using our best strategies to get what we want. God may ask us simply to stop and wait. I know He has asked that of me, many times. This is not idle waiting but an act of obedience and surrender. In other situations, we may need to turn from treating others according to the world's ways and start loving our neighbors. It might look like forgiving where we were holding a grudge. It might mean to serve where we once only wanted to be served. It might mean finally committing to a covenant community instead of isolating from other Christians who could offer accountability, help, love, and fellowship. It might mean turning from relational neglect with God to daily communion with Him as you start prioritizing regular time in the Scriptures.

Where might you be stepping outside the path of God's already revealed will in order to make some specific situation come to pass? What Ebenezer might you be trying to force God's hand to build? We've all done this to some extent or another in life, but in this season, what is it for you? Take a moment to name it—if there is one. (If not, good for you!) Now that you've named it, take in this refreshing truth: *in all seasons, turning away and repenting from our need to control is the pathway to true freedom. Surrendering to God's good and perfect will is something that will genuinely change you as a person from the inside out.* No matter what it is for you, no matter how far down the wrong path you've gone, no matter how many Ebenezers you've tried to build that just aren't going to be part of your story, it's time to turn around, friend. Back into the gentle leading of the Father. Time to step back into alignment with God's will, releasing our white-knuckled grip on control and putting the reins back in the only hands that can handle them. Because God has other Ebenezers in store. *Because God is good, and God is good to you.*

Looking Up

I still remember the pain that came with not getting that job I was so sure about. The surrender process—it took all day, back and forth with God, wrestling over the fact that I had been told no, again. In the heartbreak and tears, I finally and fully surrendered my need to control, the need to find my worth and value in my doing over my *being*. And I learned that abiding in Christ is much sweeter than our striving; trusting God's heart is much better than surviving.

That particular job was never going to pan out. It just wasn't one of those stories where God was going to pull through and give me what I wanted. And looking back, I realize that had I followed my plan, or forced God's hand to build that job-Ebenezer in my life, I'm not sure where I would be today. God didn't write that season of my life the way I would have written it, but in surrender I got to the other side, and though I don't have all the answers for that no back then, I know that the assignment I have right now from the Lord is a good one and one I wouldn't be enjoying if life had always shaken out the way I thought it should.

Now that I think about it, this has been true in so many steps of my vocational journey. I didn't even start the journey as a church girl. I was set on being an entrepreneur. But back in 2010, rather than becoming the businesswoman I'd always dreamed of being, God called me into a new place with a new passion—to serve women and meet them with the unchanging truth of the gospel. I surrendered the self-made Ebenezer of "businesswoman" and made my way to Charlotte, North Carolina, where God had other Ebenezers in store for me.

There I met my husband, Mario. I fell in love with local church ministry. And God's will came to pass. I can't say the future Ebenezers God has for your story will look like mine. Nor do I think we can say a certain marriage or job will be the reward for our obedience. But I can say this with full faith now: God's will is always better than our way, and He will always prove Himself good to us on the other side of our surrender.

I've had to go through that surrender-wrestle with God so many times from then until now. And I've finally discovered something wonderful—after enough times of doing it, I've changed. For me, *surrender is no longer "Here God, fine." It's "Here God, I trust you." And that right there is its own Ebenezer moment.*

I don't know what self-made Ebenezer you really want to be part of your story. But I know this: the Ebenezers God wants to build are better for you. A rejection is really just His redirection. Look to Him, trust Him, and surrender, friend. Because His will is better. It really is. I know it takes so much courage to turn from the path we are trying to blaze and stones we are trying to build and return to the path God wants us to walk down. I know it feels impossible to turn our gaze. Our eyes are so often down, obsessing over our own path. And they should be up, looking for His will instead and living in line with His Word. God is making a way, dear friend. He's brought you this far, and Jesus will keep you, protect you, love you, and walk with you as you let *Him* build the Ebenezers *He* has in store for you. God loves us so much that He will close the doors we want to keep open so that we can see that ultimately there was something better all along.

Let us walk forward, not by our way but by His will.

EYES UP

Lift your eyes and look back on your own journey, taking the time to chart this crucial moment (or season) in your life.

1. Can you remember a time when you surrendered a "would-be" Ebenezer stone to God in favor of His plan instead of your own? What was that like? How did this moment of surrender ultimately lead to God's will for your life?

2. When it comes to God's will, what insights of this chapter surprised you? Encouraged you? Challenged you?

3. What Ebenezer stone might you be trying to force God to build in this season? Why do you think you are trying to force God's hand to move?

4. In this chapter, we explored the ways both Moses and the king of Israel handled God's revealed will to them. What's the big difference between the two? Why is this difference significant?

5. If you are outside of God's overall will for His people— meaning, if there are ways your life is not squaring with Scripture—what would "turning around" look like for you? How can you take a step toward that today?

8 | The Cornerstone
God's Not Holding Back

O ur family is . . . just a little different from others."

I am nervous, and the words just aren't coming. My oldest girl, Leilla, is doing a school project on our family tree and needs pictures of my childhood. The thing is, I don't have anything to show her: no photos, no knickknacks, no heirlooms, nothing. My heart sinks. I knew this day would come when I'd be forced to confront the realities that although I'd tried to live a comparable life to the people around us, I would ultimately always come up short to the status quo. Comparison is the thief of all joy, as they say, because it's the doorway to discontentment. It's the key that unlocks the longing we all have to be enough and have enough.

"I'll try my best to find some, love. I think Mommy only has a few pictures." Naturally, this response jolts her into a landslide of questions. She's inquisitive, wanting to piece together who her mother is so she can better understand herself. I stand there, instantly consumed by shame, thinking about the other families and children. They will have something meaningful and beautiful to show when they present, and Leilla will not.

I feel a reluctance I know she can sense. Unpacking something so tender and nuanced isn't the most enjoyable thing to do, but it's always necessary. During one of the most complicated years of my mother's and my family's lives, we ended up losing most of our family photos and treasures. They were gone—I had nothing to give Leilla. The few tokens and keepsakes I once treasured had been thrown away.

I sit down on the couch that night with my hands covering my face. The tears won't stop flowing. Shame—this is what I feel. Deep shame for what was and what now is.

I wasn't enough for my daughter, for my family, for life.

I spiral into a landslide of comparison. It's easy to get distracted by what you don't have if you aren't practicing thanksgiving for what already is. *"God's brought us this far."*

I think about the people living a life less complicated. I compare their gifts and favor to my life—to me, who lives over here in a world of bitterness. The subtle yet powerful lie rears its ugly head in my heart: that the deck of cards has been carelessly handed to me. It lives at the core of my thoughts, shaping how I view everything around me. Somewhere along the way in my life, it became my core belief. *I am not enough, and what I have is not enough. That woman over there got it better than I did.* The better family, the better job, the better personality, the better body, the better gifts, and better opportunities. The better everything.

Comparing our false gods to one another is like comparing two cubic zircons, debating over which one is better, when none is actually a diamond. Comparison is always about sizing up two fake things instead of focusing on the real thing. We don't know it, but when we compare, we are using our broken cisterns to try to carry water pulled up from a dried-up well.

What comes to mind when you think of *abundance*? For me, for so long, it was all the stuff *she* had. Now "she" isn't just one person. Over the long haul of life, she has been a lot of different people. Her face changes from season to season. A school friend. A gym friend. A mom friend. A ministry friend. Some random gal on the Internet. Maybe you can relate. Regardless of the season of life and the specifics of the situation, I'm always tempted to find her and convince myself she's got it good while I've got it bad. She's got abundance overflowing, and I've got empty hands.

But that's the thing. What is abundance really? Sometimes I think we want abundance more than we want abundant *life*—you know, that thing John 10:10 speaks of. And by wanting "abundance," I mean we want her stuff. Her talents. Her marriage. Her kids. Her influence. Her intellect. Her body. Her friends. Her bank account. Her effortless casual outfits and glorious hair and flawless skin. Her freedom. Her job. Her education. Her status. Her binder full of family photos. And the more we obsess over those things, the more we get confused. We get confused because we don't realize that those things might look like abundance to the world, but they aren't the same thing as abundant life. The longing we have for abundance isn't a need for more or better things but to be loved, seen, and valued. It's a deep cry that longs to be told that we have a role to play here, that our lives matter, that our broken pieces don't define us, that we are a part of God's story somehow, and that our lives, these stories we tell, are a part of something more.

I want to be the mom that shows up with a photo book of memories, but I am not. I'm really the mom who's rebuilding and restoring, taking pictures of this life and piecing them together for the next generation of our family to see. I'm a living stone (more on that in a second), with a story to tell that gives hope and light. I'm not her, over there, managing the stuff she has to manage. I'm me, right here, taking care of the stuff *I've* been given to manage. And the truth is, all of us are walking testaments to God's grace and good, with good gifts, with a life intentionally entrusted to us.

You're a Stone, I'm a Stone

Comparison is a tricky thing, isn't it? How can we be sure God will "help us this far"—that He will show up to *our* lot in life—when we feel like our world is so different from hers, that person whose story is all we want but can't have? How can we know God is with us in the moments we wish He had given us another life? Another set of talents? Another part to play in His kingdom? Is He so busy showing up for her life that He doesn't have time to show up for ours? Has He been doling out the good stuff to those at the front of the line so that when He gets to us He's empty-handed?

How can we trust God will meet us in the moments we are caught up in comparison? And what would He say to help lead us out of that obsessive place?

He'd tell us this: *we are all stones*. We're all part of a greater story, a greater building He's constructing, and we all have a part to play in it that matters in its own way. More than that, when it comes to "me versus her," He'd tell us that although our lives may be different in so many ways, the truth is that *we are actually not all that different.*

Let me tell you what I mean by looking at 1 Peter 2:4–5:

> As you come to him, a living stone—rejected
> by people but chosen and honored by God—
> you yourselves, as living stones, a spiritual
> house, are being built to be a holy priesthood
> to offer spiritual sacrifices acceptable to God
> through Jesus Christ.

Did you see that? The Bible calls the church "living stones" (1 Pet. 2:5).

But what does this mean? Well, back in the Old Testament, God used to dwell in a physical place—a temple made of natural stones. But now, because of Christ's work and the Spirit's presence, we see the New Testament build on this idea of stones, telling us that *yes,* God still dwells among His people in a temple, but this time the temple is not a physical building made of physical stones. Instead, God dwells in a *living* temple: His people. His multiethnic bride. *We* are his temple! His new "house" is His people, the church. Just as He dwelt in a temple before, He dwells in it now, but the stones look different. The stones aren't literal bricks. They are people. I'll say this again: His presence now dwells inside His church, which means He dwells inside you and me. We are stones to help others remember who He is, and to be remembered, as well.

Why does this matter? Because understanding that you are a stone who is part of a bigger building changes everything. And it can seriously help you understand comparison issues in a whole new way. *What kind of stone are you in the temple of God?* Sometimes I think that instead of answering this question and being the stone we were built to be, we start looking at other stones. We start looking at *her.* Maybe she's a bigger, flashier, gem-like stone, and we consider ourselves smaller, unimpressive, or ordinary. Perhaps she seems like she is an integral part of the church's work, while we sit here day after day in our same tedious job or changing the same dirty diapers. We obsess over the blessings He seems to be giving the other stones out there, or the way He made them, and we start believing and entertaining the thought that we aren't as significant as they are. We compare someone's stone—someone's life—to our own instead of taking our place in the building. This trap hems us up to live outside of fully experiencing who we are in Christ, looking at our earthly riches instead of the heavenly ones.

We cannot know who we are if we do not know whose building we are a part of. A stone strategically placed here, in this part of the church and the temple, for such a time as this.

Friend, your life is a stone that others get to see as a signpost for the love of God. So is hers. You're a stone. She's a stone. I'm a stone. But here's what happens sometimes. We are too busy looking for more to fill us up when everything we need in life has been fulfilled in Christ Jesus. We look around at how God has fashioned or gifted *her* and get frustrated when we don't have the same brilliance or texture, the same density or color.

It would be easier for me to tell you to accept the fact that she's a really nice stone and to call it a day because God chose to make her that way, and therefore we should rejoice in the gifts He's given. But it's not always that easy; it's not always that clear-cut. And there is an undeniable feeling deep within us that needs someone to whisper words of truth and hope: *not every circumstance is a gemstone, but you are.* Sometimes what we see around us may be the thing we want—the prayer we've been praying. But this is when we have to remind ourselves of the simple truth—that we aren't called to live by the standards of the world; we aren't called to live for love but from it. Not for what we have but whose we are. *God made you a stone in His house. He gave you a place. That's beautiful. He wouldn't have brought you in to His household if He didn't love you.*

And He wouldn't have brought her in if He didn't love her, too.

Her, you, me—we're all little stones that come together to build the house of God. The whole church, each of us gathered into one body, is where God Himself dwells. She might be on the left side of the house while you're on the right. She might be teal, and you might be dusty rose, *but you're both stones. And you know what snaps you out of your comparison faster than anything?* The fact that although we are all stones that house His presence (and that's amazing!), *we ultimately aren't the point or the big deal.*

Think about it. The only reason little stones can come together and build anything at all is because there's a foundation under them, holding them steady. That's something builders call the cornerstone. And there's a reason the Scriptures call Christ the Cornerstone—*because the whole church is founded on and held up by Him*. We're built on top, sure. But we're little pebbles coming together who would have no shot at staying in tact if He weren't below us, lifting us up.

He's the big one. He's the flashy one. He's the gem. He's the foundation. He's the reason we're steady. That's the point.

In *Mere Christianity*, C. S. Lewis put it like this: "The church exists for nothing else but to draw men into Christ." We are living stones pointing to the cornerstone, and as God builds up in us a new identity, He's also piecing back together the once shattered pieces of life.

I'm a stone. She's a stone. And friend, *you* are a stone, a good one, a needed one, a beautiful one. And although it may not feel so pretty on the outside, that's okay—on the foundation of Christ who holds us up, God uses busted and broken people to build a masterpiece.

That Crazy French Guy and His Masterpiece[2]

I love a good story, don't you? They give us windows into experiences, painting pictures out of words for the moments we lack them. And the story about Raymond Isidore is one of my favorites. He was a Frenchman in the 1900s, and he famously created "La Maison Picassiette"—The House of a Million Pieces. When he was younger, he had a job as a molder, but eventually (because of medical conditions, some say) he ended up becoming a sweeper at a cemetery. As he walked to and from work, or just around random places, he would notice what the world considered trash—little pieces here and there of rubble in potholes and shards of colored glass in the dump—and he started gathering them, one by one. Jagged edge by jagged edge.

People thought he was eccentric, crazy even. For the first seven years, he focused on the interior and covered all the walls and floors with those bits and pieces the world threw out. He even included the furniture! Eventually he moved outside and created a wall, a chapel, and a throne. He even used these little bits of debris and pebbles and colored glass to create Christian symbols throughout the property. The whole project took him thirty years to complete as he added to the mosaic, piece by piece, giving each little shard its place in the greater work.

Though the townspeople thought he was an odd guy, they were amazed when they realized that he had pieced together all those little slivers of rubble to make a magnificent house. And people still visit that place in France today! The dwelling place of a true artist. A monument to remind the world of what a true artist can create with shattered, separate pieces. To remind the world that beauty can always come from ashes and, given the Christian symbols in his work, that God is in the business of rebuilding.

Friend, you and I are God's masterpiece. We are little pebbles the world might not look at and consider flashy, but when we're pieced back together by grace and glory, we testify to an artist who is bigger than all of us. Each life, a story and monument—one that cannot be duplicated or impersonated.

God chooses the unlikely and makes a *masterpiece* out of them. He literally *calls* us this: "For we are God's masterpiece. He has created us anew in Christ Jesus, so we can do the good things he planned for us long ago" (Eph. 2:10 NLT). But we are not a masterpiece because one little pebble over here is any

better than that one over there. The point isn't each pebble.
Nor does it make any sense whatsoever for two little pebbles
to bicker and fight over who is the most attractive or which
has the better part to play. The point is—*this is the house where
God dwells when the stones come together. And when the world
looks at the house from afar, it can't really see the individual
pebbles anyway, just the beauty of the whole. That's the beauty of
the church.* It's you and I, broken beings being fully perfected
by a perfect God who dwells in our midst.

Just look at how Paul talks about it in Ephesians 3:10
(NLT):

> God's purpose in all this was to **use the
> church to display his wisdom in its rich
> variety** to all the unseen rulers and authorities
> in the heavenly places. (emphasis added)

Another translation says the individual, diverse, different
members of the church reveal "the multifaceted wisdom of
God" (AMP).

Isn't that amazing? The point of each stone in God's
church is not to point to itself but to point to the multifaceted
God we serve. In other words, *you need her*—whoever "she"
is in this season—to be a little different from you. That way,
together, you show off the different parts of God to a watching world.

The church is a hospital where all people get to come
and experience a glimpse of heaven. The more I've seen this
fleshed out, the more tender I've become toward God's church,
His *ekklesia.* A people willing to love others unarms the pride
found in comparison. We start living for God when we notice

the work of His hand and heart in us and through us as the hands and feet of that hospital. As we love God's people, and take in all the different and glorious things they reflect about Him, it leaves little room for looking at the lack. When we choose to look at one another this way, we can become the hospital we're supposed to be for the weary, sick, lost, and abandoned—a hospital for souls needing saving. God did not hold out on love when He gifted us His Son on the cross and a new family that we get to be a part of. And as living stones building up His church, we get to do the same, extending the invitation to others to behold the cross and come into the family.

We're all like Raymond's house of a million pieces. When someone passes by, they aren't enchanted or impressed by that one shard of glass under the doorknob. They aren't looking at her hue of teal and your hue of dusty rose. They are amazed by the whole thing, and more than that, they are in *awe of the man who dwells in it and put it together himself.* When glorifying God in all that we do becomes our priority, our reason to breathe and to live, comparison begins to slip away because all you can think about is how good God has been and will be. When we find common unity in Christ, our Cornerstone who holds up all His little living stones, we find abounding grace within one another.

The Cornerstone

Have you ever realized that the world tries to find ways to gather around a common goal, but somehow it always falls apart? The world tries its best to get a bunch of random people and build them into an organization or a fan base or whatever, but even if it works for a while, eventually it stops working. We find this to be true in our political parties, our denominations, our gym classes, our special clubs—just to name a few. And as good as those sometimes can be, we end up failing if we try to make it hold the weight of all our hopes and dreams—because the bond we're looking to keep us together is one that can't be found in those commonalities. The cross of Christ, and His resurrection, is a better place to look, for there is where we find our unity as His people. There's not a stronger foundation under anyone else to hold us up and hold us together.

What are you trusting to hold you up? What are you trusting to bind you and "her" together in a way that won't fall apart when the pressure of rivalry or fatigue or frustration or jealousy starts bearing down on the bond? What are the two of you standing on, anyway? Nothing can bring us together and keep us together the way a good foundation can. And as we mentioned before, the Bible calls that kind of thing a cornerstone. If you and your teal-pebble frenemy over there are being put together into a house, or forced to stand side by side even when it's hard, I'll ask you again: What exactly is holding you up? Keeping you steady? If the answer isn't *"Christ our cornerstone,"* friend, it is shaky ground.

Take this in with me because it's such a balm to the soul:

> Now, therefore, you are no longer strangers and foreigners, but fellow citizens with the saints and members of the household of God, having been built on the foundation of the apostles and prophets, Jesus Christ Himself being the

> chief cornerstone, in whom the whole building,
> being fitted together, grows into a holy temple
> in the Lord, in whom you also are being built
> together for a dwelling place of God in the
> Spirit. (Eph. 2:19–22 NKJV)

The cornerstone is the first stone set in the construction of a masonry foundation. As the first stone laid, it becomes the reference point for all other stones laid after it—every piece finding its definition and position in this one piece—the cornerstone. It gives the whole structure integrity and stability, and without it the structure will fall. Jesus is that cornerstone for us. He's what we stand on. He's what holds the house up.

The cornerstone, as I said before, gives you a reference point as you keep adding stones, so you can make sure things are going in the right direction with the build or so you can know if you are deviating from the original intent of the structure. So, if Christ is not only our foundation but also our reference point for how we're supposed to be interacting with other stones, *how is that going for you?* In the way you treat your fellow stone—even the one you compare to—is Jesus's example your reference point on how to behave toward her? How did He behave toward those who seemingly had more than Him? Who were dealt different cards? Who didn't have to go to a cross?

He died for them! He went low so they could be raised up high. He was humble; He was generous; He was *for* them. Imagine how different the house could look if each stone took those cues instead of trying to rip out any pebble that shined brighter than they do?

Christ being our reference helps us see when we've lost sight of His hand at work in His house placing each person exactly where He wants them. If that's you, I feel for you. I've been there too. And you know what? Christ our foundation and reference point helps us find our way back home—back to our original design instead of trying to take on *hers*—when we are swayed by our emotions, when our feelings tempt us to redefine love or settle into pride, or dwell in discontentment. *That's* how God shows up for us in moments of comparison. He reminds us of our Cornerstone, helping us stand on Christ once more and align our lives with His.

He's Not Holding Back

I can imagine God pointing to a hollow place in the wall of His house, bidding you to come take your place. I can't know what exact place that is in the scheme of things, but I *do* know you've got one. Problem is, we're hesitant. We have this natural suspicion that God's holding out or holding back when He gives us our part to play. We go to lift our foot, and we waver: *Is that really the best spot for me?*

Friend, turn the volume up on these words right here: *If Jesus is the cornerstone holding you up, then He can't be holding you back.* He wants you to take your place in His household, and He wants your little dusty-rose self to shine right where you're supposed to be, whether it's under the doorknob or next to the windowsill or up on the chimney. He wants you to experience His love and be found in Him as He guides you to your place.

So, what's your spot in His family? Where do you fit in the blueprint? What's your story? What sphere of influence has God placed you in that reaches into lives no one else can reach? What's your gift? And how can you offer it fully and freely without trying to make it identical to someone else's? Remember, if Jesus is the foundation of the church, and if He appoints us each to our place within it, then He didn't make a mistake in your life or calling versus hers. *You're a stone, she's a stone, and we all need to take our place for this thing to hold together.*

A story in John 21 helps me think more clearly about this whole discussion around comparison and saying yes to the lot God has for us. Peter was treading along, following Jesus. But toward the end of the story, it looked like Peter and his friend John, one of Jesus's other disciples, were going to part ways. They were given different commands, told different instructions, had different futures in their kingdom work. Peter was to feed Jesus's sheep—that much was clear. Peter was also told what death would look like for him in old age, many years from then. After telling him these things, Jesus says something He says to us all:

"Follow me." (John 21:19)

You'd think the next thing we'd see is Peter moving forward, but here's what happened:

When Peter say him [John], he said to Jesus, "Lord, what about him?" (John 21:21)

Peter doesn't walk forward, following Jesus. He stops and turns around, trying to gauge what *John's* fate was. Instead of taking his place in the plan, he wonders what John's part is. *But what about him?* How many times have we done this, right along with Peter? *I know You want this or that for me, but what about her, Lord? I won't walk forward in Your commands of me until I know she's gotta face something as hard as me. I won't walk forward unless I know that I'll eventually have it as easy as her. I won't walk forward until I know her story isn't better than mine.*

We turn from Jesus and we look around, don't we? Just like Peter.

Peter is focused on God's plan for John, but here's the best part: Jesus helped him return to the plan God had for Peter. He sees what's going on, and He knows Peter needs a perspective shift about John:

> "If I want [John] to remain until I come,"
> Jesus answered, "what is that to you? As for
> you, follow me." (John 21:22)

Jesus was clear: *it doesn't matter what John is doing or what My plan is for him. Maybe I want him to stay alive all the way until My second coming, or maybe I don't. What is that to you? But I've told you the path for your journey. You follow Me. I have a place for you in My story, and you can either take it or totally miss it as you sit over there and obsess about John.*

What is it to you, Peter? Oh gosh, *what is it to us?*

A moment of comparison and insecurity had crippled Peter. These words pricked him, leaving him unsettled.

"Am I not enough?"

"Will John get a better ending to his story?"

"Did I get the bad end of the bargain?"

"Does Jesus really know what He's asking me to do?'

"When it comes to my part to play in the story, is Jesus holding back?"

Remember, Peter was looking right at Jesus when this conversation started. But then he turned around. Peter had taken his eyes off Jesus—off the call, off the mission, off his lot. And we do that all the time, don't we? We get our orders from Jesus, and then we turn around. We shift our gaze.

Here's the thing: comparison is a symptom of idolizing something we've placed on the throne of our hearts, clouding our perspective, and moving our affections to what we think should be. Can you relate to this? Do you feel it? Here's the bottom line and the reminder we all need: *We can't follow Jesus and obsess over what we think is lacking at the same time. We can't focus on the bounty if we're worshipping the lack.*

What is it to us if "she" has something different? What is it to us if what we've been given isn't the same as someone else's? What if we believed our lot in life is holy ground? We have to believe that apart from God there's nothing better out there for us. We have to believe that exchanging our one true God for little counterfeit gods is the basis of comparison over-all—and we have to go find what that counterfeit god is and chuck it out the window. *Our God is good to us, right here in this place He's put us in His house. We belong. We have a place. We are assigned a space to fill. That is enough.*

Friend, I don't know what your specific part to play is
in God's greater story. But I know this: you are not getting
a lesser version of God's grace but a whole portion of it when
you choose to follow His call. No matter what kind of stone
you are, you must remember: God's not withholding His love.
He's not holding back. If we know that God is good, that His
character is holy and trustworthy and kind—that He gave us
a place in His family—then what could He be holding back?

God is not out for behavior modification; He's looking
for soul transformation. He's not wanting you to simply stop
comparing but for you to be set ablaze on mission, loving God
and His people (more on that in the next chapter). Don't allow
the discontentment of life to rob you of the contentment found
in Jesus. It may feel like God is holding us back, but He's really
moving us forward in Him and His story. He's enough in us.
There's no need to compare. No need to look around. No need
to live from lack or scarcity because at the end of the day, it
doesn't matter what we have or what we look like. It doesn't
matter that our story isn't as tidy as someone else's. The world
elbows its way into certain circles that way, resting on all that
stuff as foundational reason for belonging, but that's not how
it works in the household of God. You're a stone—you have a
place in His house—because He met you and He saved you
and He set His love on you in Christ, regardless of all that
other stuff. *Jesus is the place you rest for your belonging.* You
didn't convince God that you deserve to belong due to your
wit or your beauty or your picture-perfect life compared to
the next girl. He made you a living stone that is held up by a
stronger foundational than what the world rests on, *and you
belong because you're* found in Christ, and Christ alone.

Looking Up

Together, you, me, her—and all the other believers in this world—are a masterpiece being built by God. We're His house, where He likes to dwell. *Do you believe that?*

And Christ is our Cornerstone, the one holding us up so we can take our place in the family. So we can belong. So we can play our part, regardless of the part someone else is playing that feels like a threat to us. And instead of a threat, the truth is, we need those stones over there—whoever they are, whatever their life looks like—to play their part, or the whole house won't be as strong. *Do you believe that?*

Friend, when you begin to doubt these things, eyes up on the One who calls you a living stone.

When you begin to think God's holding back, cast your eyes to your Cornerstone—the One who's holding you up and could never hold you back.

When you begin to think that she has it better, remind yourself that you've been entrusted with a place in the family to steward. And that place matters. Remind yourself of Jesus's words to Peter: *What's it to you how I lead her? You follow Me. You take your own place in My family. You be faithful with the lot I've given you. She needs you to be faithful with your square inch, and you need her to be faithful with her square inch, so the house can stand strong. So get to your space, and fill it up!*

And when the struggle still looms large, or reemerges in your heart when you thought you had finally overcome it, take heart: *He has met you at every other place in your journey. He will meet you in the hard moments of comparison, too. He will meet you even there. And He will remind you of the truth.*

I want you to take a moment to let courage and hope overflow. Ask yourself this question, Where along the way did you forget that God gave you a place to belong, a space to take up in His family? When did you forget He has gifted you with good things—that He made you that dusty-rose stone on purpose? Have you ever believed it? This space right now is to sit in what might be a place of tension for you, a time to trade in unmet expectations or comparative thoughts for *God's* dreams, for *God's* plan for your place in His house. A time to give God space to redeem the parts of your heart that once allowed comparison to rob it of its joy, its identity, its mission.

Because mission? Oh, friend. You've got one. Yes, you do.

EYES UP

Lift your eyes and look back on your own journey, taking the time to chart this crucial moment (or season) in your life.

1. When has God met you in a difficult season of comparison? How did He meet you in it?

2. In this season of your life, whom do you compare yourself against the most? Why?

3. Why is it crucial to understand Christ as the Cornerstone who holds up all His people? How does this truth change things as you face battles with comparison?

4. In this chapter we learned that each believer in God's church is a little living stone, built together to make a dwelling place for the mighty presence of God. Explain why this reality is so significant in our struggles with comparison.

5. In this chapter we looked at John 21:19–22; Ephesians 3:10; 2:19–22; and 1 Peter 2:4–5. Which of these passages was most impactful for you? Why?

9 | Multiplying the Stones
Your Purpose, His Mission

I 've got a close friend who's more like a sister. We'll call her Layza. For most of her life, Layza lived with a deep sense of emptiness, wondering if she'd ever have a meaningful role to play on this side of heaven. No mission, no purpose. There had to be more to life than her nine-to-five job, than the sleepless nights with the babies, than cooking and cleaning and sleeping. Than the tension and the hurt.

Throughout her childhood, she sensed that something was just off. She didn't fit in, didn't have the sense of family and belonging that she assumed a child would. As she became older, she noticed this feeling was getting stronger, unshakable.

One day she thought to herself, *Could I be adopted?* There was no real indicator that this was a possibility, except for maybe a few things she'd noticed—not a whole lot of baby pictures and the feeling that something was just not right.

Fast-forward a few years. Layza came to find out that she was, in fact, adopted. Her world suddenly came to a stop. We met over lunch soon after to process and pray. She was undone. My soul sister, crushed from the weight of life. This all seemed so meaningless. Where is the purpose in this? Why wasn't she told earlier? What did that mean about her history? Her past family? Where were they now? What in the world happened all those years ago? The questions and the uncertainty of it all flooded her like a tidal wave.

As we processed together, we made space for the pain. For the loss. For the shock and the sadness. And with something like this, *of course* room should be made for the shadow side of such an ordeal. But at the same time, Layza would tell you she eventually came to realize that sometimes we lose sight of the fact that the lives we've been given are God gifts to steward. We forget that under our two feet is holy ground, filled with divine appointments sent by God. That ultimately, our stories—Layza's and yours and mine—are God's plan, His hands and feet to be the walking testaments of His riches and grace. And over just-okay pizza on a mundane day, I rallied around my friend Layza to affirm this truth over her heart and mind. I helped her not only remember what was true but stand up strong on it when the tidal waves threatened to take her down. Because that's what I would want if the roles were reversed— and honestly, sometimes, they are. Sometimes I need her to remind me of the truth when I face my own versions of "shock and awe" in this life. And so we sat there, and as the confusion whirled around us, I reminded her of something a mentor had recently said to me:

"It may not seem like your life has purpose now, but your life *is* filled with purpose. Not because of who you came from or what memories fill your story but because you are filled by Jesus. Your mission is to bring others along to see Him and embody Him in their everyday life. And when we experience a trial, it becomes an opportunity to be a testament—an Ebenezer. All we have to do is let God build it."

Our stories aren't always like Paul's "road to Damascus," where we encounter that one powerful or dramatic moment that defines our life forever afterward, where we're brought low to the point of blindness or confusion and, at the same time, given a glimpse of glory. Our moments in this life aren't always full of this kind of pain and suffering or intensity. They won't look the same or feel the same. And even if we do endure the hard moments and make it to the other side, it's not like we get an automatic guarantee that what is waiting for us on the other side is fame or fortune. In fact, that's typically *not* waiting for us on the other side of hardship. But you know what all these moments always have in common?

They are all set apart. Each with divine purpose.

Layza's story has been one of the most impactful things I've ever witnessed in my life. I saw her tell her story. I watched her resolve to believe that God was good. I caught a glimpse of what it looks like for a woman to trust that God was redeeming her past just as surely as He was meeting her in the present, and let me tell you: it was a gift to behold. Layza holds empathy like I cannot; she cares more intentionally than anyone I know; she loves her children with a fervor that moves all who watch. She's strong and long-suffering, quiet yet confident. She is the aroma of gentleness and loyalty, and all who know

her know Jesus more because of her love. She serves with reckless abandon and shares her heart as a way for people to see
Jesus. Layza's life, although full of trials and tribulations that
deserve to be grieved and tended to gently, holds a gift to con-
nect with women whom I may never relate to, but that doesn't
matter because it's a gift God clearly meant to give *her*. Layza
gave me the gift of knowing God through a different lens, all
because she shared her story with me, her testimony.

And you know what? *You are a Layza in somebody's life.*
Your story could be the single most impactful thing for them
to witness. Because our stories—yours, mine, Layza's, all of
ours—are a doorway for onlookers to see God's redemption
and love. Even if you're in the middle of the story. Even if
you're in a part of the journey that doesn't make sense. I mean,
aren't we all in the midst of God's work? If I had the chance
to take your hand right now and look you in the eyes, and
I would say this loud and clear: *your story of Ebenezer after
Ebenezer—it isn't just for you.* It's for others, too. Every page
of it was written by God so that you might believe He's good,
yes, but also so that someone else might catch a glimpse of His
goodness, too. *Your story matters. Your testimony deserves to be
shared. It was written with a purpose, and you have no idea how
God might want to use it over just-okay pizza or coffee or whatever, to change the lives of the people around you.*

So in the short remainder of this book, we're going to talk
about that. About using your story. And on top of that, we're
going to talk about your place in the mission of God as you
walk out of this book and into the world. Because that place
is waiting for you. It is. And the way you discover your part

to play in the mission is by *telling your story, naming your gift, finding your place, and multiplying your Ebenezers.*

Tell the Story

Friend, you've looked up throughout this entire book, casting your eyes to the ways God has shown up for you over and over again. Even in the places you once believed His hand wasn't at work. You've seen God build your Starting Stone—where God first began to stir your heart toward Him. You've seen God build your Stone of Knowledge—where God revealed more of Himself to you through His Word and His people. You've seen God build your Living Stone—where you came to faith in Christ! You've seen Him carry you from one season to the next. Care for and love you.

And there's more. You've seen Him build stone after stone after that, haven't you? Your Grieving Stone, where He met you in the sorrow. Your Mountaintop Stone, where He helped you in the heights. Your Gravestone, where you thought your faith had met its end, but He guided you out in faith. Your Stone of Surrender, where He helped you turn from a path you were trying to force so that you could find your way back down the path He had for you all along. Your Cornerstone, where He met you in the battle with comparison and helped you stand together with someone you once felt insecure around, so that you both might take your place in God's household.

This dear Friend, that's *your* story. Those are *your* unique Ebenezers that no one else but you and God can call your own in the specific ways they played out. No one else has that same story with those exact details. And God meant for that to be the case. That's your story with Him.

And your Ebenezer story is powerful. It gives you something to fall back on and remember when life gets hard. But you know what? The purpose of your story is about more than just finding fresh faith in tough seasons. As we just discovered, it's about other people, too.

Like I said before, you've been looking up to your Ebenezer stones during this journey. And that's good because it showed you your own story. It showed you how to trust God's heart by tracing His hand in your life. It taught you how to cast your gaze upward toward all that He's done for you, especially in the moments when life gets hard. And I'm so proud of you. You've spent so much time looking up in this book. *But now it's time to look around.*

All these Ebenezer stones you've watched God build throughout this weren't built for just one person to see and enjoy; they were for a community of people to witness in order to remember God for who He is and recall the ways He's worked. And that's important in our day and age. I've learned that many don't want to argue about facts these days; they want to see how God makes a difference—how He's real in someone else's life. Sharing your Ebenezer story with others helps them tangibly trace God's hand and heart when they may be in a season of spiritual fog. It helps them see fruitfulness in barren seasons. It helps them see that God really does work in the lives of His people, and He really is good—and good to them.

In a postmodern age, our stories are our most powerful weapon. And you, friend, you carry a sacred story. You carry words and experiences. You carry love and pain that someone needs to know. Our stories are messy, beautiful, multifaceted masterpieces. They all are. Your stones of remembrance, your life as a living stone helps your faith community and the lost community around you too, the people entrusted as your field to love. The Ebenezer story God has helped you chart in this book helps all those people see in living color just how active God has been in your life. And more than that, it gives them hope that He is just as active in theirs, if they'd only take the time to look up.

> Who in your life is caught in their own difficult season?

> Who in your life is saying the same thing you used to say: "God is good, just not to me?"

> Who needs to learn what tracing His hand looks like so that they might trust His heart?

> Who needs to chart their own Ebenezer journey and, in doing so, finally discover the God who has met them all along?

I don't know what faces are popping up in your mind right now, but I do know this: they could use an example right about now, couldn't they? Imagine—it might be that they need to hear your Ebenezer story for fresh faith. It might be that they don't know God at all, and your testimony is the very thing God will use to open their eyes to the fact that He's good, and He's working, and He shows up for people who call out to Him.

I love how Psalm 107:2 puts this: "Let the redeemed of the LORD tell their story" (NIV). Or in another translation: "Let the redeemed of the LORD say so" (ESV). Let them tell their story. If God has redeemed something in their life, or built an Ebenezer somewhere, let them *say so*. Whew.

You are redeemed. *God has met you*. And through this book, you've built a map of your whole story which proves that's true.

Use it. *Say so*.

Name Your Gift

With living on mission and being living stones in the family of God comes discovering the God-given gift that dwells within you. Apart from our experiences and God moments and Ebenezer stories, we also have gifts imparted to us by the Holy Spirit. It's supernatural and beautiful. You were built for a specific purpose and created with specific gifts. Spiritual gifts show up in various places, but for a quick overview, let's look at Romans 12:6–8 (NIV), which lists a few of the gifts for us:

> We have different gifts, according to the grace given to each of us. If your gift is prophesying, then prophesy in accordance with your faith; if it is serving, then serve; if it is teaching, then teach; if it is to encourage, then give encouragement; if it is giving, then give generously; if it is to lead, do it diligently; if it is to show mercy, do it cheerfully.

Each of these gifts fleshes out differently in each person but, when realized, are easily noticeable to you and those around you. They help us come together as one body to support the bride of Christ—the church. No one gift elevates one person over another. Every gift matters and plays an important part, although society and the flesh try to tempt us to believe that some are unimportant. In fact, some parts of the body that would be considered weakest or least important by the world's standards are considered indispensable to God (1 Cor. 12:22). Others' abilities will make up our deficiencies. That's why we all need one another, each member of the body showing up and doing her part. God does not give us gifts to create our kingdom but to build up His.

To steward these spiritual gifts well, I believe there are a few things that we must keep in mind.

- We must realize that all gifts and abilities come from God. Every good thing, even our borrowed breath, is for His glory (James 1:17).
- As we live from our identity in Christ, who we are and our natural gifts will become clearer. There will be no need to fabricate or bifurcate.
- Not all of us will have the same gifts, and that's beautiful. That's what makes us need one another and lean on one another!
- The gifts come from the *Spirit,* not ourselves. That may sound a little basic to

you, but a lot of times, pride in our own abilities happens because we tend to fall into thinking our natural abilities are the real source of our spiritual giftedness, and that's not the case. *God is the source.* As 1 Corinthians 12:4–6 says, "There are different kinds of gifts, but **the same Spirit distributes them**. There are different kinds of service, **but the same Lord**. There are different kinds of working, but in all of them and in everyone it is **the same God at work**" (NIV, emphasis added). "All these are the work of one and the same Spirit, and he distributes them to each one, just as he determines" (1 Cor. 12:11 NIV). If you have a spiritual gift, you didn't muster it up. The Holy Spirit distributed it to you for a purpose.

• Speaking of purpose, the aim of spiritual gifts is not to draw attention to ourselves or to serve ourselves. The purpose of the gifts isn't really about us at all. It's about others. Spiritual gifts are given to serve other people and build up the church. The Bible puts it this way: "Now to each one the manifestation of the Spirit is given for the common good" (1 Cor. 12:7 NIV). Not *your* good but the *common* good. When you don't use your gift in the context of your faith community, you're not robbing

yourself of a chance to be noticed; you're
robbing the common good of the church!
Others miss out when you don't own your
gift and use it! They need your gift just
as much as you need theirs. We must be
willing to use our gifts wholeheartedly,
not holding any good thing back from
serving and loving others because at the
heart of it—this is mission at its core.

God's gifts differ in nature but never in effectiveness. He
will use our little and do much with it! Our role is to be faithful and serve others using the gifts God has given us.

Friend, you are sitting with God-given gifts that His
household needs. And although wildly different in function,
they are all a part of a puzzle, with a specific placement and
shape. And like every puzzle, each piece always had its place;
it's just our job to find where. It's sort of like that house we
talked about in the last chapter. You might be a little stone
under the doorknob while your friend is by the window. You
might be dusty rose while your friend is a teal blue. The point
is not exactly how we compare against our fellow believer. The
point is to find what our place is, what our gift is, and use it
so that the house might be stronger as a whole.

So friend, what's your gift? Name it. Right now. And if
you're not sure, ask God and then ask some godly believers
in your church who know you well and can speak into your
giftedness. Whatever shape it takes, your gift is there. Name it!

Find Your Place

I want to help you reframe what finding your place looks like. I'll start with this—God has already built the table you need to be at and pulled up the chairs. In the kingdom of God, no one is left out. In the kingdom of God, there is no room for putting stakes in the ground to mark our territory. In the kingdom of God, we don't prove to find our place; rather we place ourselves as God's vessels to do His work. You aren't out here looking to see where you fit in but where God has placed you—where He's revealed a need to you. And it's here we begin to see some of how God is inviting us into mission. And more often than not it's more obvious than we think.

As we were chatting in the last chapter, God has made you a living stone in the household of God, which means He has a place for you.

So, how do you discover where and how to show up and live on mission? The simplest answer is this—serve your church or community with your Ebenezer story and your spiritual gifts. This may look different depending on the season of life that you're in but will always serve to build up God's kingdom.

Take Acts 6:1–7 as an example. The twelve apostles were out and about spreading the gospel. But a new need arose. There was a daily distribution of food set out for widows, and in the flurry of women trying to get their food, a certain group of widows was clearly being neglected. So, what were the apostles to do? They couldn't do two jobs at once. As the church increased, new needs were clearly increasing, and they had to come up with some sort of solution. So the apostles had

to find some kingdom workers who had both the character
and the gifting to handle this new need. When we read along
in the Bible, we see how they settled the matter:

> "Brothers and sisters, choose seven men from
> among you who are known to be full of the
> Spirit and wisdom. We will turn this responsi-
> bility over to them and will give our attention
> to prayer and the ministry of the word."
> This proposal pleased the whole group.
> They chose Stephen, a man full of faith and
> of the Holy Spirit; also Philip, Procorus,
> Nicanor, Timon, Parmenas, and Nicolas from
> Antioch. (Acts 6:3–5 NIV)

Look at that—new kingdom workers taking their place in
the household of God! People gifted to serve were serving, and
people gifted to teach and preach were teaching and preaching. All needs were being met because all hands were on deck.
And look at the result of this:

> So the word of God spread. The number of
> disciples in Jerusalem increased rapidly, and
> a large number of priests became obedient to
> the faith. (Acts 6:7 NIV)

When people step up to their place in the church, whether
they are gifted in mercy or service or teaching or otherwise,
the Word of God spreads rapidly, and people start obeying
God. People start to experience the love and kindness of Jesus.
People see the kingdom of God right before their eyes. All
because people were willing to use their gifts and take their

place in the family and the mission of God. All because people were willing to show up at the intersection of *gifting* and *need*.

Friend, it might not be a situation with widows (or maybe it is!), but there is undeniably a need in your midst. Ask God to show you where the need is and use your gift there. That's how you find your place in the family of faith and the greater community. Mission is less about doing and more about being. Because when we are with people, we get to witness to them. Our being is our witness. Wherever you find your place, find it with people. Where is the need in your midst?

Mission is not the work we do; it's how we tend to the work of hearts and how it meets our hands. Mission is not something we construct or create; it's something we live out. Mission is partnering with God to try to set things right on this side of heaven through Christ's power and presence in and through our lives. It's living for the cause of Christ and His people and not our own.

It's never been about how much we can do for God but our willingness to show up fully with grace in one hand and compassion in the other. It doesn't have to be formal. It could be something as simple as walking with someone through the fire. It's phone calls and meals. It's Bible study and groceries. It's encouragement and hope. It can be serving in the nursery on Sunday morning or serving in the nursery of your home all the way through the night when your baby needs your tender touch. It can be joining the worship team or turning on the worship channel in your car when your lost friend needs a ride to the airport, letting her hear some warm encouragement and truth, and asking her what she thinks about the lyrics. It could be formally teaching a women's Bible study in your local faith community or informally teaching the friends in your workplace who Jesus is in those in-between water-cooler moments during break time. It could be packing lunches for the homeless or packing boxes in your warehouse job at Amazon while you pray for your neighbors. Mission is all that and more. But no matter where it is, what it looks like, or how formal it is, *you have a gift to use, and you have a need somewhere in your midst, and you have a space to fill.* Find your place by identifying that need and jumping in.

Multiply Your Ebenezers

You're an ember, waiting to catch fire for those who need the light, the warmth, the spark. This message is just that, a movement of hope and resilience, to multiply the God stories and spread the good news that met us, saved us, and changed our lives. Often it's easier to sit in the rut of life. That place feels comfortable to us, doesn't it? Safe.

But what if I told you there's a world around you that needs someone to help them see their story? What if the fog is too thick, what if their eyes are fixed on their own brokenness instead of the body of Christ broken for them?

As I said before, you've learned how to chart your own Ebenezer story in this book. And I encouraged you to tell that story. Now I'd like to go one step further—teach someone else to chart out her story, too. Help her build her Ebenezer stories. Pass down what you've learned here in this book. Others need it just as much as you did, just as much as I did when God helped me chart my own story. Teach someone else how to cast her eyes up and map out her own story, so that more and more of us will worship with one voice the God who met us, who calls us, who makes us a unique part of His story.

Friend, multiply the power that comes with mapping out your own story and show someone else how it can make a difference in her life as she leans into it and shares it with others. Just imagine a movement of people with their eyes up, knowing without a doubt that their God has met them at every juncture of the journey. *We'd be unstoppable.* And more than that, God would be glorified and worshipped as good and *good to us.*

You, my friend, are the vessel for this upside-down kingdom on this side of heaven. And your stories? The Ebenezers? They are a tangible display of God's affection and love. Your pain and your healing, your turmoil and your peace, your hard and your holy, all for His glory. Do you feel it? The conviction, the fire within? That's the love of Christ in you. And God's Word tells us that the love of Christ compels us to live on mission, to share our story and the story of the cross that has changed us forever. The love of Christ compels us to leave behind whatever we once considered the prize and run toward Jesus as the true prize. The love of Christ moves us to be ambassadors of His story—one that has intersected with ours in such a deep way that it can never be untangled—ministers of His name and messengers of His reconciling gospel (1 Cor. 5:14, 19–20). For love of the God who met us and changed us, we go forth and multiply our story.

There's no greater call, my friend. No greater thing to be a part of. For the love of God, multiply your story.

Looking Up and Out

It's no mistake that on my birthday I am laying down the last heart words of this book. The words became a message and movement years ago. The words that saved my life, rescued my heart, and redeemed my soul. The words that helped me walk through the tensions of the seasons where reconciling hard things with a good God didn't make sense. And I pray with everything in me that God will do the same for you with them.

This is the part of the book, the time of your life, when you stop and realize the beautiful story of grace that's been gifted and set before you. This is when you step back and begin to see the wonder and way-making power of Jesus. It's when you learn to see God and remember God. Where you find yourself moving past wondering if God is good, or present, or here, and begin to live from the resolve that *He is.* That He has met you this far, over and over again, and He won't stop now.

Your life, your story, every hard and good thing being held by God and given new purpose. I hope you see that have you're not too far gone. I hope that today you see that God's doing a new thing. I hope you see God as a Father who loves you, as God who's always cared. I hope you know that this isn't the end for you, that if anything, God may just be getting started in your life. I hope your Ebenezers, as you look back at them, fill you with wonder and awe and hope, not just for your past but for your future. Because you have one. And in Christ it is glorious.

What we encounter on this side of heaven will not make much sense, until one day it will. Until we realize that it has never been about a linear path in one direction but more of a journey where we learn to love and see and heal for His glory, our good, and the good of others. Like the Samaritan woman, who dropped her jar and ran to tell those in the village about a man who knew everything she ever did, will you also drop what you've carried, what you've known, the shame that's held you back, the weight, the strongholds that once defined you? The trauma, the past, the fear, the betrayal, the unforgiveness, the performance, the guilt—will they become Ebenzers? Will you let God's hand touch them? Will you "say so" (Ps. 107:2)? Will you tell of the God who met you and brought you this far?

I believe with everything in me that these words will be seeds sown, little crumbs left for you to look back on. I pray that they are the vessels of light that break through the darkness, getting the attention of your heart, slightly turning your gaze toward Him. Where there was once a marker of barrenness, you now also see God's faithfulness. This is your Ebenezer.

It's far past time for you to tell your story, to name your gift, and to get to work in the place God has for you. It's time to see your life as God has always seen it. It's time to heal, to grow, and to go. Share your story, how God met you in seasons of darkness. Share how you're still in the middle of your healing, but a good God's strength and living water have kept you through the wilderness. Share your beginning, middle, and now—because we need to see all of it and God in it. We've got nothing to lose when we've found everything we need in Christ. And when we lose sight of God's hand, may we retrace the Ebenezers, lifting our eyes to them, remembering that we can always trust His heart. He met us back then. He has met us this far. He will meet us again. And He will meet those who come to know Him through our story.

Because God is good, friend—past, present, and future. And God is good to you.

Eyes up.

EYES UP

At the conclusion of this book, think back on your entire Ebenezer-stone story, and thank God for the different ways He has met you along the way.

1. Look through the chapter titles throughout this book. Which stone in your story was most impactful for you? Why?

2. Who in your life needs to hear your Ebenezer story? Why do you think you hold back from sharing it?

3. In this chapter, we explored spiritual gifts, and we were encouraged to name our spiritual gifts. What is yours?

4. We learned in this chapter that one way to find our place in God's mission is by identifying a need in our midst. What need(s) are in your faith community right now? How might you meet this need?

5. How might you multiply your Ebenezer story? Who in your life might need to learn how to chart their own story the way you learned to chart yours?

6. What's one major lesson from this book that the Lord is impressing on you? How can you walk forward with eyes up toward that lesson as you exit this book and enter the mission field around you?

Notes

1. Spurgeon's original wording is this: "The Christian believes God to be too wise to err and too good to be unkind! He trusts Him where he cannot trace Him. He looks up to Him in the darkest hour, and believes that all is well." See https://www.spurgeon.org/resource-library/sermons/a-happy-christian/#flipbook/ or https://ccel.org/ccel/spurgeon/sermons13/sermons13.ix.html.

2. The details of this story were provided by "La Maison de Picassiette: Raymond Isidore," *Spaces*, accessed December 8, 2021, http://spacesarchives.org/explore/search-the-online-collection/la-maison-de-picassiette.